MIDLAND RED
BUS GARAGES

Malcolm Keeley

Ian Allan
PUBLISHING

First published 2013

ISBN 978 0 7110 3690 1

© Malcolm Keeley 2013

Published by Ian Allan Publishing Ltd, Hersham, Surrey KT12 4RG.

Printed in Bulgaria

Visit the Ian Allan Publishing website at www.ianallanpublishing.com

FRONT COVER 1960 C5 coach 4798 at Evesham had been relegated to C5A dual-purpose status with bus blinds but still benefited from the black roof livery when seen in late 1968. *Ken Jubb*

BACK COVER Although this is Stourbridge garage, forming one of the town's bus stations, D9 5399 belonged to Hartshill, operators of most journeys on the 245/6 to Wednesbury and Dudley. Midland Red held on to 5399 when the PTE took over, possibly believing it to be the last D9 built completely at Carlyle Works. Actually that honour belonged to 5400 which did pass to the PTE – the remaining D9s, 5401-45, had their bodies finished by Willowbrook. 5399 in time passed to the Transport Museum, Wythall, where many readers will have enjoyed a nostalgic ride on it. *Ken Jubb*

TITLE PAGE This conductor outside Sandacre Street garage, Leicester appears to be wondering if the No Admittance sign includes him! The date is 7 May 1966 and the bus is 4844, an ex-Kemp & Shaw 1950 Leyland Titan PD2/1. *Andrew Willis*

ABOVE Birmingham's Digbeth garage shortly after opening in 1929. The office block took account of the future line of the highway and looked rather strange in splendid isolation. The road was eventually widened in the 1950s.
Courtesy Stockholm Transport Museum

CONTENTS

INTRODUCTION

There was so much enthusiast interest in Midland Red's vehicles that Ian Allan's ABC fleet books ran to eleven editions. The Birmingham & Midland Motor Omnibus Co Ltd (the proper name of Midland Red – usually shortened to BMMO, both used indiscriminately throughout this book) also published its own fleet list and we eagerly awaited the next pink-covered edition, issued absolutely free. The Ian Allan version, however, contained a full list of bus services and a map. This meant that you had the basic information to deal with the other item of irresistible interest listed within – how to visit every one of the company garages. Enquiry offices supplied the details and your passport was the 'Day Anywhere' ticket, reintroduced in 1958, just in time for me to take advantage of them.

Visiting every garage was the best way to see every bus yet even your author in his youth missed one – S12 3761 at Hereford. When I saw Hereford garage in 2011, I realised that, somehow, I had never been there before and I was correcting an astonishing omission after fifty years. Not surprisingly 3761 was no longer there but ironically I'm able to include a picture of it within these covers.

All those garages and enquiry offices, not necessarily located at the garages, were taken for granted. At the company's peak after World War Two, the garages accommodated around 1,800 buses and coaches, covering 12,000 square miles with route mileage of around 6,500 miles - a total of 1,150 separate stage carriage services running into 15 counties. In addition to the buses required for these, the company's garages maintained, in exemplary condition until NBC days, the large fleet of coaches for cruises and long-distance express services.

Midland Red was a company that moved a million passengers each day. Its services varied widely in character and the crews seemed to relish the grand cycles of routes organised by the schedulers to maximise efficiency. There were many intensive urban services that provided the income to keep the whole, massive empire afloat but the company is more romantically remembered for its rural rides, serving villages so small that the speed limit signs were almost back-to-back. Country residents required Birmingham or the nearest market town while, travelling the opposite way, townies looked for peace and fresh air. On these country routes the crew might have said "And they pay me to do this!" Town or country, however, neither looked so promising when the snow shovel was required or the local river was in flood.

A lot has been written about Midland Red's vehicles but in this book the emphasis leans towards the company's property development and hopefully will be a small tribute to the work of the BMMO Architect's Department. Garage capacities upon opening are generally quoted but it must be remembered that the buses of that time were only around 26-27 feet (8 metres) in length.

Much of the detail on the garages was gleaned from the wonderfully informative Staff Bulletins (the staff magazines of Midland Red) that ran a series of articles in the early post-war years entitled "Around the Garages" and "Spheres of Influence". Paul Gray also kindly presented me with the results of his obviously considerable amount of dedicated research on the company's properties during which he evidently gained

LEFT S9 3424 loads in Angel Place, Worcester, outside the company's Booking Office and Travel Bureau, leased from June 1926; one of those magical places where for many years you could buy a day ticket to anywhere – perhaps a slight exaggeration by Midland Red. The clock, bearing the company name, was firmly attached to the building and, although the office has closed, the clock remains at the time of writing. *Ken Jubb*

BELOW Midland Red's operations around Dudley were particularly fascinating. Several garages served the town and many routes were shared as a result of geography, availability of garage capacity, and trade union protection of members' interests. The Bus Station around Fisher Street was filled with the company's buses; here 1953 BMMO D7 4099 waits to take up its next journey in the summer of 1970. *Ken Jubb*

an unhealthy interest in rating revaluations (a sure sign that something had occurred). Paul's work reminds us that Midland Red had other properties, most importantly Carlyle Works in Edgbaston, Birmingham. There were enquiry offices in towns both with or without company garages but also staff hostels plus quite a few dwellings acquired with land and rented out (almost invariably described as cottages which sounds deceptively rural – a bus garage outside the back garden was the reality!) Mike Jordan identified a number of properties largely blotted out by buses on photographs, spotting often tiny distinctive features with a skill that a crime scene investigator would envy.

Other thanks are due to Peter Jaques, who tirelessly sought out answers to numerous queries and contributed masses of additional information, and to the Kithead Trust. The photographers have been generous and informative with a special vote of thanks to Ken Jubb without whom this book would have been much poorer. So many others have contributed valuable nuggets or assistance, including John Breen, Tim Brown, Mike Greenwood, Martin Hobson, Mike Holloway, Stan Letts, Lloyd Penfold, Jeremy Price, Paul Roberts, Graham Stone and Roger Torode – apologies to any others I have accidentally omitted.

Those inspired to learn more about the vehicles, allocations and operations of Midland Red will find a number of books available, including several by Mike Greenwood and myself, published by Ian Allan. Additionally I am pleased to acknowledge and recommend the following information sources for this book:

Midland Red Volumes 1 and 2 by Messrs Gray, Keeley and Seale published in 1978 and 1977 by the Transport Publishing Company.

Midland Red fleet histories PD2 and PD3 published by the Omnibus Society and PSV Circle in 1961 and 1959, and subsequent fleet histories PD19, 20, 21 on Midland Red North, West and South published by the PSV Circle between 1991 and 1993.

'Round the Hills', by Christopher Davis published in 1979 by the Omnibus Society.

Midland Red Allocations and Fleetlist (vehicles 3000-6473) by Tim Brown published in 2008 by the Birmingham and Midland Motor Omnibus Trust, Wythall.

Midland Red fleet histories published by L Simpson, the Midland Red Enthusiasts Club.

Midland Red's Railway Inheritance, article by Peter Jaques and Christopher Davis in the March 2008 Newsletter of the Roads & Road Transport History Association.

Stratford Blue by Robert Telfer published in 2003 by Tempus Publishing Ltd

The more you think about the hard work building up and maintaining this fantastic company and its properties, how annoying it must have been to have to hand over a whole chunk to the West Midlands Passenger Transport Executive in 1973. That the new owner probably could not fail to show how unimpressed they were by the rundown state of the acquisition no doubt rubbed salt in the wound. And imagine the sadness when the rest was broken up into separate companies in 1981.

Malcolm Keeley
October 2012
Solihull

BUILDING MIDLAND RED

The British Electric Traction Company Ltd (BET) was formed in 1896 to develop electric traction throughout the country and was soon a major player in the industry. Against a background of BET's near monopoly of tramway and horse bus operations within Birmingham, a private company, the Birmingham Motor Express Company, Ltd., was formed in 1903. BME was undercapitalised so it floated a new company, whose shares were to be available to the general public. This was the Birmingham & Midland Motor Omnibus Company, Ltd., registered on 26 November 1904.

Unfortunately little interest in the fledgling company was shown and it failed to raise sufficient capital to acquire the BME assets. Agreement was reached to merge Birmingham Motor Express with the BET's horse bus assets in Birmingham, and the dormant BMMO was used for the merged businesses. The transaction was backdated to 1 June 1905, the agreements were signed and shares issued on 21 July, and BMMO commenced operations in its own right as a BET subsidiary on 15 August 1905.

BMMO, with Orlando Cecil Power as its Traffic Manager, not only took over the double-deck motorbuses operated by BME but also the 100 horse buses and 1,000 horses previously operated around the city from various premises by the City of Birmingham Tramways and the Birmingham & Midland Tramways. There were also four motorbuses that CBT had put into service to compete with BME. The maintenance of the motorbuses proved a continual problem and, on 5 October 1907, the survivors were taken out of service and horse buses restored in their place.

The Tilling-Stevens petrol-electrics selected for the reintroduction of motorbuses in 1912 worked out of a garage in Tennant Street, Birmingham. O C Power showed great loyalty to his horse bus drivers; the lack of gears on the Tilling-Stevens chassis made it easier to retrain and keep the men in employment. This time the motorbuses were a success and carried a colour familiar on BET-owned horse buses in the city – bright red. The initial Tillings carried the BET magnet emblem on their flanks but the 1913 buses were the first to carry the fleetname 'MIDLAND'. The Midland "Red" legend had begun. All existing horse bus routes were quickly converted to motorbuses and, during 1913, local services commenced in Smethwick, Oldbury and Sutton Coldfield.

On 5 September 1913 Birmingham Corporation opened an electric tramway along the Hagley Road and BMMO had to divert its buses. Negotiations led to the highly successful agreement between BMMO and Birmingham Corporation dated 14 February 1914, whereby the company would not compete with the Corporation within the city boundary and the Corporation would not compete with the company outside. This involved the purchase by the Corporation of the company's operations wholly in the city, including the leasehold of the Tennant Street garage and thirty double-deck motorbuses, effective from 4 October. BMMO removed its headquarters to its Bearwood garage and began to build up a network of services from central Birmingham to towns and villages outside the city boundary.

World War I

The hostilities were a major blow to many bus companies who had their chassis or even complete vehicles requisitioned by the War Office. The Tilling-Stevens petrol engine, however, did not directly drive the bus through a gearbox but via a dynamo powering a large electric motor. The military did not approve of this petrol-electric system initially so BMMO kept its fleet intact. The company was thus able to step in when associated companies had to withdraw facilities, acquiring developed bus services and facilities to maintain the buses used on them. As a result, Midland Red vehicles began to work from garages at Kidderminster, Worcester, Warwick, Nuneaton and Twogates near Tamworth.

Post-war Expansion

Hostilities ended in November 1918 and BMMO set about consolidating its wartime gains and expanding into new areas. Following the successful agreement with Birmingham, the company began negotiating arrangements defining areas of operation with other local authorities.

The years after the war saw a period of intense competition. Many men had been released from military service with experience of driving and maintaining motor vehicles, surplus examples at reasonable price being within reach of the ordinary man for once in his lifetime as he received his war gratuity. Many truck, bus and coach operators began around this time. It is widely painted that an established operator like BMMO had to fend off these fiendish pirates. BMMO, of course, had only begun its outward march from Birmingham at the outset of the War so one should have as much sympathy for the small man endeavouring to make a living in a totally deregulated environment. BMMO had the advantage of size and the financial backing of the BET group.

It was an era of fearless investment and dynamic promotion of the company's services. It was the practice for a few buses, with the necessary staff to man them, to be despatched to a selected town and a network of routes built up with the minimum of facilities. Competition would be challenged, and, where practicable, eliminated. No mileage was dropped as long as a reasonable return could be obtained. Additionally, the company began seasonal regular long distance services from Birmingham to coastal resorts in 1921, the first services being from Birmingham to Weston-super-Mare and to Llandudno.

The company opened further garages all over the Midlands throughout the 1920s but BMMO faced stiff competition in some of the areas it moved into. The company's Chief Engineer, Mr Shire, concluded the company needed a lightweight, reliable straightforward design of bus, combining the capacity of its Tilling-Stevens single-deckers with the nimbleness of the small buses operated by the competition. Manufacturers could not provide such machines so Mr Shire decided that BMMO should build its own. BMMO was fortunately in the middle of an area geared to the needs of the motor industry and he was already sourcing items from the numerous engineering workshops. Shire completed his first bus in 1923 and its high revving performance with plenty of power is credited as a very important step in the evolution of the British bus. Shire designed for just his company, however, giving him latitude denied to other vehicle makers who had to compromise to meet the varied requirements of the commercial market. For the next half-century Midland Red designed and built nearly all its own bus chassis, frequently more advanced than the big manufacturers, and the bodies too from the mid-1950s.

By now the tramways of sister BET companies in the Black Country were suffering from independent buses. Although BMMO had deliberately refrained from competing with BET-owned tramways, this permitted other operators to abstract the traffic and, from 1924, Midland Red vehicles were sent in to operate over the tramway routes and give the opposition a run for their money. From 1926 onwards, Midland Red buses began to replace the various tramways. Other bus routes were rapidly developed to create a network of fiendish complexity and consequent necessity for extra garages. Away from the Black Country, Midland Red buses helped dispose of the Burton and Ashby Light Railway in February 1926, replaced Worcester's trams in June 1928 and the Kidderminster to Stourport tramway in November 1928.

By the late 1920s, Midland Red possessed what looked like a marvellous network on the route map but, in reality, the frequencies were often thin, in some cases market days only.

The big four railway companies had gained powers to operate bus services in 1928 and this really caused the big bus groups, like BET, to break into a sweat. Until then they had been able to crush much of the competition but suddenly here were potential rivals with similar financial muscle. Fortunately the railway companies decided on a different route by approaching major bus companies and buying into them, thus sparing a wasteful fight. On 24 April 1930, the Great Western Railway and the London, Midland & Scottish Railway purchased half the ordinary shares of the BMMO company. The most visible change was the revised title on company notepaper which now read "Midland 'Red' and Railways Joint Motor Services". The Great Western Railway, a pioneer bus operator in its own right, possessed a few services and these were merged into Midland Red services between 1930 and 1932.

Regulation

The Road Traffic Act, 1930, brought regulation to the bus industry through the close control of Area Traffic Commissioners who, before granting road service licences, took into consideration representations by persons already providing transport facilities along or near a proposed route. Operators who obtained such licences thus enjoyed the protection of the Traffic Commissioners. Gone were the days when independents could poach on the company's best routes, and similarly Midland Red could no longer use its superior might to crush the opposition. Between 1931 and 1939, more than 150 small businesses would be purchased by BMMO to consolidate the company's network. As the fleet size crept beyond the thousand mark, extra vehicle accommodation became necessary and more garages were opened through the 1930s. Most were handsome structures with brick fronts decorated with stone dressings but some were simply steel frames with cladding, probably where the need to get accommodation into use was really pressing.

Important purchases, effective from the end of June 1935, were two companies of the Midland Counties Electric Supply Company and these were operated as subsidiaries for the time being. One was the Leamington & Warwick Transport Company, which had by now replaced its trams with buses. Midland Red buses would take over in 1937. The other was Stratford-upon-Avon Blue Motors Ltd., operating under the fleetname Stratford "Blue", with whom Midland Red had agreed a working arrangement in September 1932. This delightful company with two garages was retained as a subsidiary for many years.

War and Peace

The outbreak of the Second World War in 1939 saw the fleet standing at around 1,300 vehicles with great effort having been taken throughout the company's growth to extend or add to the garage stock and ensure the best quality maintenance. All coach cruises ceased at the end of that season for the duration

The globe above the registration number was known as a 'leopard spot', fitted to all the pre-war vehicles. Different coloured and patterned spots identified the garage maintaining the vehicle, the space to the right being used when the bus was loaned to another garage. 'Leopard spots' started to fall out of use from around 1944 and were officially abandoned in 1949. *BMMO*

of the war. There were serious cuts in services, with railways covering the long-distance requirements, soon followed by a huge growth in demand to factories involved in the war effort. Bus production across the country ceased completely for a time. Despite the essential role of buses in getting people to the factories, the military requisitioned parts of several garages. Mr Shire thus faced the double frustration of being unable to build new buses and told by Lord Beaverbrook that his excellently accommodated rolling stock could be run from fields, roads and waste ground like the military. He retired in 1940 at the early age of 55, being replaced by Mr Donald M Sinclair who became General Manager shortly after the Traffic Manager, Mr Power, passed away in 1943.

The buses were subjected to continuous heavy overloading. In 1939 BMMO had carried 210 million passengers but this had increased to 327 million in 1944 with the buses operating two million less miles. The war effort caused shortages of maintenance staff, components and other materials leading to make-do-and-mend ideas to keep the buses on the road.

The years of peace after 1945 saw the restoration of the facilities that had been curtailed and also a travel boom while

From 1949, one inch high two letter codes were added to the left hand side of new destination blinds, usually the first and last letters of the town the garage was located in - many readers will be able to rattle off the code for each garage rather more easily than identifying the leopard spots. On the post-war buses, the top roll of destination blinds was known as the 'A' blind and the lower the 'B' blind. Early post-war buses up to 3406 also had an 'A' blind at the rear. The traditional garter crest was featured on the rear emergency door of S6s when new in 1946-7 and surprisingly retained on S6 repaints for many years. 3088 was transferred to Nuneaton in September 1959, where it was seen in the town's bus station in 1960, and remained allocated there until withdrawal in November 1962. The NN code can be seen on the left of the blind. *Ken Jubb*

new housing estates created a demand for increased frequencies and new services. Where possible, double-deck vehicles were introduced but the fleet size increased by a quarter. A major programme of building and extending garages was undertaken to cope, largely designed in-house with a clear architectural style. Progress in providing the additional garage space was perhaps the slowest of all the post-war problems to solve, obtaining licences for the building construction being a laborious and frustrating business.

Garages had lorries to take worn-out items to Carlyle Works for replacement or repair, and bring home new or reconditioned engines, gearboxes, spare parts, seats etc. BMC FG models formed a later generation of trucks, including these two seen at the Works in 1970. 7956 HA was badged as an Austin when new in 1963 - WHA 282H stands behind. *Ken Jubb*

Carlyle Works and Midland House

Such a large company had to maintain its vehicles and needed a central overhaul works. Midland Red, however, went further and designed and built its own vehicles between 1923 and 1970. It was therefore very proud of Carlyle Works, a site of approximately seven acres off Carlyle Road, Edgbaston, Birmingham.

The company took over buildings from Daimler Co Ltd in September 1920 and began carrying out body repairs and overhauls there. The remainder of the site and buildings were taken over in November 1924 and production of the company's own chassis moved from Bearwood garage shortly afterwards. Capacity constraints meant that chassis and engine overhauls and new engine manufacture remained at Bearwood for the time being, not an ideal arrangement. Plans were thus drawn up during World War Two for everything to be concentrated on the Carlyle site. Early post-war building licensing constraints and materials shortages delayed plans but reconstruction work began in 1947. The completed complex was proudly reopened as 'Central Works' on 25 November 1954 as part of the company's Golden Jubilee celebrations although many continued to call it 'Carlyle'.

A large and handsome 1860s building of red brick with stone dressings in Vernon Road, Edgbaston, Birmingham, conveniently adjoining the Carlyle Road works, was purchased in October 1952 and renamed 'Midland House', increasing the combined site to eight and a half acres. This became the registered offices of the Company in 1953, although the Traffic and Staff Departments remained at Bearwood for nearly twenty years longer.

Golden era ends

Passenger figures peaked in the mid-1950s at almost 500 million per annum but then began to drop as more and more people were able to afford private motoring, while the impact of television slashed evening traffic.

Staff shortages since World War Two were initially thought to be due to the early post-war shortage of housing. The company purchased premises in Leamington, Sutton Coldfield and Dudley for use as staff hostels. Sadly staff shortages became chronic as the company failed to compete with buoyant industries such as vehicle manufacturing with better pay and more sociable hours. The transfer of some services to Birmingham City Transport in 1957-8 provided a bit of relief, easing shortages of staff and garage space. The continuing strong competition for labour meant younger skilled engineers were tempted elsewhere and BMMO found it difficult to replace the craftsmen who had spent their lives with the company and were now retiring. From 1962-3, increasing numbers of Leylands and Daimlers had to be bought to supplement the falling output of new BMMO vehicles. Many BMMO buses from the mid-1960s had their bodies completed by Plaxton or Willowbrook and complete buses of outside manufacture formed an increasing part of the new vehicle intake as engineering staff concentrated on maintenance and overhauls. The reducing production of new BMMO vehicles became hopelessly uneconomic and the last BMMO bus entered service in June 1970.

The distribution of vehicles on page 10, after the takeover of Brown's Blue, Markfield in the late winter of 1963, reveals how little work the coach fleet did out of season. As well as buses and coaches, the fleet included dual-purpose vehicles of bus outline with improved seating that normally ran the longer bus services but could assist the coach fleet at times of pressure. Dual-purpose buses, however, lacked adequate luggage capacity for coach services. A new designation therefore from 1966 was the semi-coach which was vehicles used on bus services during the week but had sufficient luggage space to perform weekend coach duties, allowing coaches underused on weekdays to be disposed of. The stopgap measure in 1966 was to reclassify forty C5 class into this role but 1967 saw forty new Leyland Leopard and BMMO S21 semi-coaches.

The ordinary shares in BMMO held by the Great Western Railway and the London, Midland & Scottish Railway had passed to the state upon railway nationalisation in 1948 but the company had remained under private control with British Electric Traction. Despite openly declared opposition by Midland Red to nationalisation, with a Labour government in power that could have imposed worse terms under compulsory purchase, BET agreed in November 1967 to sell its shareholdings in UK bus operating companies to the state-owned Transport Holding Company. Thus, from 14 March 1968, Midland Red became wholly owned by the THC. The National Bus Company was created on 1 January 1969 to take control over the English and Welsh subsidiaries. BET could count itself fortunate because, from 1970, wages and price inflation increased while new drivers' hours regulations worsened staff shortages.

Stratford Blue and its two garages were finally absorbed into Midland Red on 1 January 1971. The company was now losing money heavily and it was no longer possible to subsidise loss-making country services with profitable urban routes, a policy that was annoying urban councils. Under the Transport Act 1968, county councils could subsidise rural services but there was limited enthusiasm, many routes ceased to run and four garages were closed in 1971. It is at this point the garages built by Midland Red began to go their separate ways.

ALLOCATION LIST 16 March 1963

GARAGE	Code	Coaches	Single-Deckers	Double-Deckers	Total
Banbury	BY	-	26	7	33
Bearwood	BD	14	12	51	77
Bromsgrove	BE	2	26	22	50
Coalville	CE	1	40	18	59
Markfield	CE	-	2	12	14
Cradley Heath	CY	-	16	28	44
Digbeth	DH	15	31	60	106
Dudley	DY	-	12	37	49
Evesham	EM	2	15	8	25
Hartshill	HL	-	9	43	52
Hereford	HD	1	32	16	49
Hinckley	HY	1	29	16	46
Kidderminster	KR	-	34	24	58
Leamington *	LN	4	49	34	87
Leicester Southgate St	SS	4	23	58	85
Leicester Sandacre St	SA	3	26	48	77
Lichfield	LD	2	10	6	18
Ludlow	LW	-	10	4	14
Malvern	MN	-	19	3	22
Nuneaton	NN	6	52	6	64
Oldbury	OY	1	5	56	62
Redditch	RH	1	10	23	34
Rugby	RY	2	49	-	51
Sheepcote St	SH	1	-	33	34
Shrewsbury	SY	-	54	10	64
Stafford	SD	1	7	36	44
Stourbridge	SE	-	23	38	61
Sutton Coldfield	SN	1	14	54	69
Swadlincote	SW	1	24	17	42
Tamworth	TH	1	28	14	43
Wellington	WL	1	39	-	40
Wigston	WS	2	13	31	46
Wolverhampton	WN	2	7	25	34
Worcester **	WR	6	71	12	89
Engineering Float		-	26	31	57
Stored etc		114	-	-	114
TOTAL		**189**	**843**	**881**	**1913**

* Old Warwick Road and Myton Road.
** East Street and Padmore Street

ABOVE This recalls Midland Red coaching at its best. 1950 C2 3347 was allocated to Leamington in its later years and is seen, complete with driver in white coat and cap, arriving under trolleybus wires at Bournemouth. The C2s originally differed from the C1s because they were built as 26-seat touring coaches. By this time 3347 had been upseated and was thus internally similar to the C1s but remained instantly recognisable from a C1 because both windscreen glasses were recessed.
T C Bassindale/ The Transport Museum, Wythall

BELOW It looks like an operational garage but it never was. These are premises acquired at Pensnett in the 1950s but, in the event, only used for storing delicenced coaches during the winter and withdrawn stock. This view shows sixteen C3 and C4 coaches, presumably lined up especially for the company photographer as they block the entrances. *BMMO*

West Midlands Passenger Transport Executive

The Transport Act 1968 required the NBC and West Midlands PTE to co-ordinate bus services within, to and from the PTE area. The PTE did not want an operating agreement, it preferred full control of the services. Eventually the NBC agreed that the PTE could purchase services operating totally within its area with effect from 3 December 1973, including 413 buses and the garages at Birmingham Sheepcote Street, Dudley, Hartshill, Oldbury, Stourbridge and Sutton Coldfield, as well as taking over the staff to manage and run them. Bearwood garage was closed too, Bromsgrove and Cradley Heath reopening to take on services that remained with Midland Red previously worked by Bearwood and garages now with WMPTE. On the plus side, some WMPTE services that operated beyond the West Midlands County boundary in the Wolverhampton area also passed to Midland Red.

The money from WMPTE was reinvested in the company including takeovers of smaller operators, most notably Green Bus of Rugeley in 1973, Harper Brothers of Heath Hayes the following year, and the Shropshire Omnibus Association in 1978. Property investment included new premises at Cannock and Redditch. With Birmingham no longer significant, from 29 March 1974 the company name changed from the Birmingham and Midland Motor Omnibus Co Ltd to the Midland Red Omnibus Co Ltd.

Division

The loss of the West Midlands services proved a catastrophic blow and the company limped on, ever shrinking. As the 1980s opened, it was bad news all the way for traditionalists. The regular operation of the last half-cab buses in the form of BMMO's own D9s had finished on the last day of 1979. Their conductors finished on 31 May 1980, latterly concentrated at Leicester's Southgate Street garage and the last on the system. No less than three garages closed on the same day. The long-established parcels service had ceased at the beginning of that month and the fleet strength fell below the 1,000 mark. The last BMMO buses of all, several S23s, were taken out of service at the end of February 1981. Much worse news was to come – Midland Red itself would disappear.

Midland Red evolved the Market Analysis Project whose principles were later extended widely across the industry. MAP introduced service networks covering the majority of passengers' requirements, each only using the number of vehicles that allowed each garage to be self-supporting. These free-standing networks meant Midland Red lent itself to the decision to divide it into several smaller companies from 6 September 1981.

The Birmingham-based coach operations became Midland Red (Express) with around 80 coaches. The four bus operators received around 200 buses each and had rather unimaginative names - Midland Red (East), Midland Red (North), Midland Red (South) and Midland Red (West) – use of the brackets became variable. There is one last thing the operating companies did together before such ideas became regarded as uncompetitive under deregulation. Midland Red East had successfully promoted its X limited stop services under the 'Expressway' name. The public was confused by the proliferation of names and all four companies saw the benefit of a unified image for limited stop services. Thus, on 28 March 1983, Midland Express was launched. The companies, however, were subsequently separately privatised under the Conservative government's reorganisation of the entire bus industry and have since vanished into the new large groups.

The Central Works at Edgbaston was due to close in the 1981 split but was saved by becoming a separate entity, Carlyle Works, competing commercially for coach and truck overhauls and repairs, subsequently converting vans into minibuses and constructing complete bodies. It was purchased from National Bus Company in March 1987 but difficult trading conditions caused the then owners to go into receivership in October 1991. The Works closed, the remaining assets auctioned in December (including the proud brass plaque commemorating the relaunch in 1954), and the site sold for housing.

The NBC believed in much more central control than BET and required its subsidiaries to adopt standard liveries from 1972. All coaches had to wear a white 'National' livery that looked grubby after the slightest shower. The goodwill built up over the decades by the red coaches was swept aside. The wash machine operator has to ensure a respectable result on CM6T 5674, seen in the Mill Lane yard behind Digbeth garage on 30 March 1974. The corporate livery for the bus fleet permitted a shade of bright red but bland white lettering debilitated the appearance. Garages also received the NBC lettering which generally looked neat if unexciting. *Garry Yates*

BIRMINGHAM EARLY PREMISES

The horse-drawn operations of the BMT and CBT companies had been carried on from various stables around the city, including Bearwood. Their history is outside the scope of this book and they mostly disappeared along with the horse buses. The exception was St Mary Street, Ladywood, retained as the base for BMMO's Horse Contract Department which provided horses for hire "for any period of purpose", according to the advertisement. Vans were also available on hire and horse chars-a-banc for short distance outings were advertised well into the 1920s. BMMO's last horse was not sold until 1929.

Birmingham Motor Express leased the yard of the Five Ways Inn, Ladywood Road, to garage and maintain its vehicles, and BMMO took over this arrangement. The increased motorbus fleet under BMMO caused Ladywood Road from 1906 to concentrate on maintaining and overhauling the motorbuses while the operation of them joined the horse buses working from Bearwood until the complete reversion to horses in October 1907.

The ex-City of Birmingham Tramways property in Tennant Street had been a horse depot and was acquired by BMMO in 1912 to operate the new fleet of Tilling-Stevens double-deckers that successfully reintroduced motorbuses, working on the Hagley Road and Harborne routes. Tennant Street included the Company's offices but the premises passed with thirty buses to Birmingham Corporation Tramways under the 4 October 1914 agreement. At that time Tennant Street was operating 71 buses, the remainder staying with BMMO and transferring to Bearwood. BCT continued to run buses from here and also used it as a works until the opening of Tyburn Road Works on 4

TOP The assets of horse bus operator Birmingham General Omnibus Co Ltd were acquired by BET in 1899. These are the stables in Taunton Road, Balsall Heath, in 1903. The more recently painted gate bears the name The Birmingham & Midland Tramways Ltd (Omnibus Department). *The Transport Museum, Wythall/ courtesy Peter Turner*

ABOVE This stagecoach was maintained by Taunton Road and photographed during a 'country drive' at the Stonebridge Hotel on the Birmingham to Coventry road near Meriden. The date is again 1903 so it predates BMMO. However BMMO continued to advertise for some years the availability of their four-in-hand (referring to the number of horses) stagecoaches named Tally-Ho, Magnet, and Tan-tiv-y – perhaps this is Magnet as the BET symbol is on the door. *The Transport Museum, Wythall/ courtesy Peter Turner*

December 1929. Tennant Street reopened in August 1930 as the garage working single-deck services until closed operationally after 10 October 1939. BCT (by now retitled Birmingham City Transport) then used it for ancillary vehicles until 1954.

BIRMINGHAM BEARWOOD

Transferred to BMMO 14 September 1905
Closed: 2 December 1973

Strictly speaking Bearwood garage was in Smethwick with only a very small portion of the site - on the Rutland Road side - being in Birmingham. Bearwood was among the assets passed to BMMO when it became operational. Along with other depots in various parts of the city, it was responsible for horse buses, horse-drawn commercial vehicles and other conveyances taken over from the City of Birmingham Tramways.

As noted under the early premises chapter, Bearwood briefly operated motorbuses until the complete reversion to horses in October 1907. Motorbuses returned to Bearwood in October 1914 with the staff and services not taken over by Birmingham Corporation with the company's garage at Tennant Street. Bearwood was modernised immediately, the evidence of horse stabling soon being eliminated and two-storey office accommodation provided on the Bearwood Road frontage.

The early 1920s saw Bearwood taking on chassis erection, engine building and testing, and vehicle overhauls. Adjacent property was acquired in 1923, the year the SOS prototypes were constructed. A four-storey office block was constructed with big

enquiry office display windows and more garage facilities to the rear. Bodywork construction and chassis erection were transferred to Carlyle Works in 1920 and 1925 respectively but, for the time being, Bearwood remained the centre for overhaul of all running units, including assembly of new and overhauled engines, as well as development and experimental work. Mucklow Hill was handy for the test chaps at Bearwood to give early chassis a sound thrashing. For many years, the casting, machining and forging of most principal components was contracted out to Beans Industries.

Space soon became inadequate again so in 1930 two shop premises were purchased with land to the rear, enabling further enlargement of the garage and office accommodation. Two more adjacent shops were later purchased for use as offices but only slightly modified. In addition to the Bearwood Road vehicle exits, there was later another one in Rutland Road, approaching the garage via a driveway. A house adjacent to this driveway later housed the Drivers' Training Department. By now Bearwood was a fascinating architectural collection of buildings containing a honeycomb of offices and workshops surrounding the large

LEFT Bearwood stables in 1912 with the horse-keepers before the animals were replaced by motorbuses. The picture was supplied by Peter Turner whose father Charles, then a youth, is mounted on the horse in the background. Charles joined BMMO as a fitter's boy in May 1916 earning two old pence per hour, beginning a 50-year career with the company. His father Ben was also a company employee, having been Chief Horse-keeper at Taunton Road, and the Turner family Dalmatians can be seen in the foreground – men often took dogs to work to tackle vermin attracted by horse fodder.
The Transport Museum, Wythall/ courtesy Peter Turner

RIGHT Bearwood garage around 1920. Properties to the right of the photograph were later purchased and, in 1923, redeveloped as part of the garage. *BMMO*

BELOW It may not look like a style pacesetter today but 1920 Tilling-Stevens TS3 OE 6156 was the first with this design of body, in this case built for BMMO by Birmingham Railway Carriage & Wagon and seating 32. There were no longer separate ventilators above the main side windows (see page 32) – the latter would be lowered if required to provide fresh air. *BMMO*

bus parking area. There was little change after 1935 but the site remained congested until the transfer of many departments, not least everything to do with chassis and engine production, to Carlyle Works and Midland House in 1950-3, the remaining office and administrative staff following in December 1973. The entire site was closed upon most services passing to the West Midlands Passenger Transport Executive, although the premises were used non-operationally until February 1974. The property was used for a time as a covered market before demolition early in 1979.

Bearwood particularly worked services, often jointly with other garages, to the west of Birmingham, linking the city with nearby towns, plus locals around Warley. Very interesting buses could be seen as prototype and experimental vehicles usually ran, at least initially, from Bearwood. Even after the transfer of functions to Carlyle Works from 1950, buses from garages awaiting despatch to the Works for body overhaul, and newly overhauled vehicles before return to their normal garages could be run from Bearwood. In addition to SOS and BMMO types, outside manufactured double-deckers at Bearwood included a few AD2s, LD8s in some quantity and finally Fleetlines. The M1 motorway coaches were maintained here in their earlier years.

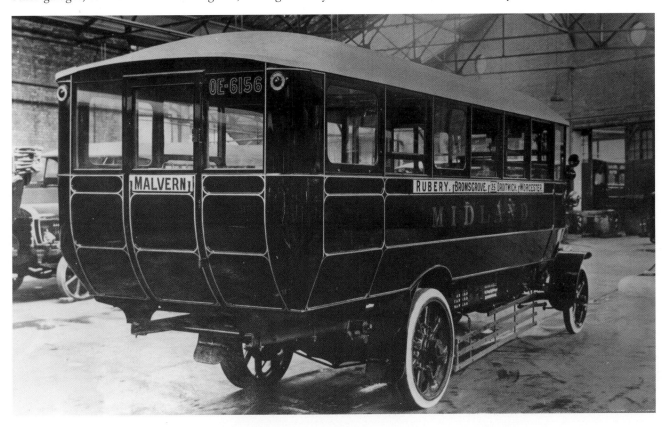

15

LEFT Looking along Bearwood Road in the opposite direction around the time of closure, showing the later extensions. Nearest the camera in a basically unaltered building is the Travel Centre as the Enquiry Office had become known. Next is the 1935 extension in white reinforced concrete, set back to a newly prescribed building line. The large four-storey block is the 1923 building with its superb rounded windows that advertised the original location of the Enquiry Office. Beyond that are the earlier buildings re-fronted around 1914. *Ken Jubb*

RIGHT A view dated 26 August 1935. The wall behind AOB 513, the 1934 Morris Oxford 16 hp saloon, was soon removed and replaced by support pillars to give greater flexibility within the garage. In front of the Oxford is training vehicle HA 2250, with RR class HA 4994 and IM4 HA 8254. The training vehicle was an extraordinary beast – the chassis was one of the Tilling-Stevens front entrance double-deckers constructed in 1923. After withdrawal in 1928, it received the engine, gearbox and clutch used in the Q ('Queen') type to begin its long career as a driver instruction vehicle the following year. In 1931 the 1925 Brush single-deck body from SOS Standard HA 2418 was converted to full width cab for dual controls and fitted to HA 2250. The wonderful creation lasted until 1952! *BMMO*

BELOW Seen at the Rutland Road entrance, HA 2453 was a member of the ODD class that comprised one 1929 prototype and fifty production vehicles built in 1930. The chassis were from the 1925 batch of SOS 'Standard' buses and the odd, in every way, classification may have stood for Original Design Development. The displaced 1925 bodies were transferred to earlier Tilling-Stevens chassis. The new 26-seat bodies were supplied by United, later to evolve into the rather better known Eastern Coach Works. They were particularly useful for quieter routes and upseated to 30 in 1934-5. Most ran until 1938 when this one was converted to a tree cutter and retained in this role until 1952. The company had a number of tree cutters, particularly important in the busy years after World War Two when many services were converted to double-deck buses. *G H Stone*

BELOW RIGHT Bearwood was home for many prototype vehicles. The first of Mr Shire's four mid-1930s rear-engine prototypes was BHA 1. The quartet was not particularly successful in this form and Mr Shire's thoughts were turning to underfloor engines between the axles at the time of his unexpected retirement in 1940. The work continued under Mr Sinclair, all four returning to service with underfloor engines by 1944 and, under a new model identification regime, soon classified S1 to S4. This is BHA 1 rebuilt as the S1 and carrying fleet number 1591. It received this unusual front end during the rebuild but a serious accident in 1952 saw the front rebuilt again to the latest specification, including power doors. 1591 was finally withdrawn in 1956. *Roy Marshall*

ABOVE The post-war prototype own-built double-decker was 2541 (HHA 1) which became known as the BMMO D1. This retained a front engine as the underfloor position caused difficulty with overall height and internal headroom. After many years favouring forward entrances under the Shire/Power regime, Mr Sinclair was convinced the rear entrance offered faster loading. The body was a considerable step forward in design, boasting concealed radiator and long windows with low maintenance sliding ventilators. The front is a BMMO design registered on 2 January 1943 under reg no 839978. Local builder Metro-Cammell would construct many bodies for Midland Red in the early post-war years but, at the time of the D1's construction, had not been permitted to resume bus production. Its partner in the MCW group, Weymann, thus built the all-metal 56-seat body. Originally open platform, in 1949 it was the first Midland Red bus to be fitted with driver-operated power doors – attracting much press attention at the time. 2541 for many years was a familiar sight around Bearwood, only moving briefly elsewhere during its trial days, and is seen leaving the local bus station. 2541 was withdrawn in December 1961 by which time post-war bus replacement was already underway. *Ken Jubb*

TOP RIGHT Until 1 April 1968 when it was decentralised, the Drivers' Engagement and Training Centre at Bearwood handled all driving tuition although drivers destined for certain districts received their final training elsewhere. With the desperate need for additional drivers in the early post-war years, the dual control tuition fleet was strengthened. Two SONs were converted in 1952 to full width cabs and dual controls for driver training, one being CHA 551. The other, DHA 696, was one of the hundred 1937-8 SONs with English Electric bodies that had tapering window pillars. It is seen in 1960 at the Rutland Road entrance to Bearwood garage, parked directly outside the company's driving school; above this was the staff canteen. *Ken Jubb*

RIGHT Subsequent dual-control trainers were based on former coaches, built from new with full width cabs. The next two trainers were rebuilt in 1955 from SOS SLR models 1980 and 1983 (CHA 962/5), new in 1937 with English Electric coachwork. CHA 962 here ran until 1963. *Ken Jubb*

ABOVE 1949 BMMO C1 coaches became available for conversion to dual-control trainers from 1961 and their underfloor engines meant bodywork modifications were minimal. 3323 was a trainer from 1964 to 1975. *Ken Jubb*

LEFT As staff shortages worsened, vacancies advertisements appeared in an increasing number of spaces on the buses themselves. Spaces were particularly available on the older buses, especially those used for training. One wonders how appealing these worn-out relics looked to potential employees. Brush-bodied FEDD 2261 (FHA 243) is parked in St Marys Road, across the road from the garage, awaiting its next victim. Most Brush FEDD trainers had the minimum work to adapt them for their new (and probably short-lived) role. This FEDD, however, has had the staircase removed and the fuel tank moved back to allow the instructor to sit directly behind the trainee driver. 2261 worked as a trainer from 1957 to 1961. *Ken Jubb*

LEFT D5B 3787 was converted to a mobile workshop in 1965 and performed this function until replaced by D7 4088 in 1969. It was allocated to the Works but is seen here at Bearwood in 1965. *Ken Jubb*

BIRMINGHAM DIGBETH

Opened: 3 January 1929

To Midland Red (Express) 6 September 1981, renamed Midland Red Coaches May 1985,
absorbed into Midland Red West 22 December 1986. Became National Express Coach Station

Still in use

The large site in Digbeth, stretching from Rea Street to Mill Lane, was purchased in July 1925 and cleared of old shop, warehouse and dwelling properties. Early correspondence refers to Rea Street garage but evolved into the familiar name Digbeth before opening. Midland Red erected a brick faced steel frame garage without intermediate pillars, the whole weight of the roof being carried on trusses. An impressive three-storey office block, including a Booking and Enquiry Office, was built on the corner of Digbeth and Mill Lane. The garage was also the company's Birmingham coach station and a passenger café followed on 24 July 1933.

Digbeth's core operations were the busy local and longer distance bus services out of the city along the Stratford, Warwick and Coventry roads. Local routes were run from Acocks Green and Solihull. The garage also contributed to the 144 Malverns, 148 Evesham, X68 Leicester and X96 Northampton – Shrewsbury services and ran more annual mileage than any other garage. The original official capacity of 110 vehicles was exceeded by the 1940s and longer vehicle dimensions, reducing capacity to 95, exacerbated the inadequacy.

The coach operations had to be suspended during World War Two but the huge boom in bus and coach passenger carryings immediately afterwards increased Digbeth's allocation even further. Matters began to become critical when the Ministry of War Transport granted operators' permission to reintroduce

A view of Digbeth as the road widening nears completion. The Birmingham City Transport 1951 Daimler CVD6 on trolleybus replacement service 58 is on the land formerly used by Midland Red for parking and also obscures a view of the Waiting Room and Enquiry Office. The roofing of the garage extends across to the Fred Purkis building. *BMMO*

long distance services from 1 February 1946 and tours and excursions from 14 April, both without limitation on mileage. Temporary use of a wide piece of land as a bus parking area in front of the garage was agreed with Birmingham City Council in 1946 but this was intended for dual carriageway widening of the street that gave Digbeth garage its name and had to be given up in autumn 1953 for the road improvement.

One of the ideas to relieve Digbeth garage in the early post-war years was to build a garage at Shirley, in the south of Solihull. Around two acres of land were acquired in Marshall Lake Road in 1947 on a 99-year lease for a new garage. Platform staff recruitment was already revealing itself to be a problem in areas of similar character, for example Sutton Coldfield, so the idea did not proceed. Thought was also given to rebuilding Digbeth as a two level structure. The opening of Sheepcote Street garage in August 1951 and the

takeover of part of the Walsall Road group of bus services by Birmingham City Transport in 1957-8 took most of the steam out of the problem.

The garage was thus reconstructed and extended as an orthodox one-level structure in 1958. The road widening had

BELOW LEFT The Short Bros bodies on the first production batch of FEDDs, new in 1934, were tired after World War Two. Samlesbury rebuilt six bodies to a rather severe style in 1948, including 1552 (HA 9414) at Digbeth garage, taking advantage of land alongside the garage intended for road widening. *G H Stone*

BELOW The Coventry service, commenced in February 1914, was the longest of the early routes at 18 miles. In the early days, it took 80 minutes in each direction but the 159, as it was eventually numbered, became fastly timed at 58 minutes (with only 2 mins at the termini), aided from the fifties onward by the dual carriageway along the A45, known to boy racers in particular as the 'Stonebridge Drag'.

100 Leyland Titan PD2 double-decks were built in 1952-3 to compensate for a shortfall in BMMO production. Many of these powerful Leylands were allocated to Digbeth and ideal for the 159. No 4031, nowadays restored and maintained at Wythall by the 1685 Group, is seen at Meriden when new. Meriden, proclaimed by a medieval cross and the cyclists' war memorial visible here as the alleged centre of England, was the principal calling point en route yet 159 buses used to show 'via Stonebridge'. A high spot of the ride, in more ways than one, was the punishing hill out of Meriden en route to Coventry. *The Transport Museum, Wythall*

RIGHT An everyday situation recorded on 18 September 1965 as increasing coach business encroached into the everyday activities of the working bus garage. The driver eyes up yet another paying customer dangerously close to the barely fenced inspection pit in the coach loading area while the punter watches LC7 Leopard/ Duple 5793 drive over it. *Andrew Willis*

established a proper street frontage and, on the corner of Digbeth and Mill Lane, an impressive four-storey building was constructed named Spencer House after John Spencer Wills, then the BMMO chairman. The building achieved a considerable degree of uniformity with the adjoining Corporation-owned flats and shops. It included modern facilities for the coach station with a spacious booking hall, ample seating accommodation and a 100-seat self-service restaurant. Attention was given throughout to fixtures, fittings, furniture, decorations and colour schemes – unfortunately the 1960s was just around the corner and tastes changed rapidly. Telephone Rentals Ltd, the tenant in Spencer House, installed the internal telephone and public address systems throughout the premises. In the coach loading area itself, an impressive façade directed passengers to the support facilities but subsequently the combination of passenger circulation and vehicle maintenance facilities under one roof attracted criticism, despite further improvements. Space to maintain and wash the bus fleet could be scarce, especially on a peak Saturday when Digbeth could be distributing 16,000 passengers on 500 coach departures.

A nearby overflow yard thus remained necessary, and was firstly located in Benacre Street. Then on 25 July 1965, a large piece of land was purchased from West Midlands Gas Board in Adderley Street, opposite Birmingham City Transport's Liverpool Street garage, and used as a parking area from 10 September. Plans were drawn up for a new garage here to take all the buses operated by Digbeth and Sheepcote Street, the latter to be closed. Digbeth would have become solely a coach station with an allocation of coaches only. History, notably in the form of the West Midlands PTE, overtook these plans.

Digbeth operated a wide variety of types but notable wartime intruders were some of the hired buses, and the austerity Daimlers that ran from here until transferred with the work to Sheepcote Street. The Daimlers had preselector gearboxes and the S3 prototype underfloor-engine single-decker 1943 was similarly equipped so it was allocated here too. Digbeth was accorded a high priority for post-war vehicles, including AD2s but these did not stay for long. Around a third of the 100 LD8 Leylands could be found here for over a decade from new in 1953, and these were joined by Leyland Leopards and Daimler Fleetlines from 1962-3.

Digbeth also operated a fleet of express and tour coaches. On 2 November 1959 the coach station was the scene of another triumph for the Company when the country's first motorway express coach, a vehicle specially designed by BMMO for the purpose, set off on its 80 m.p.h. trip down the M1. Midland Red thus introduced Britain's first motorway express coach service, although in the early days the coaches were actually maintained at Bearwood.

The Adderley Street site was included in the transfer to West Midlands PTE on 3 December 1973. Digbeth remained with Midland Red and kept its long-distance coach duties but its bus operations were profoundly affected. Most of the existing bus work was transferred to the PTE's Moseley Road garage, reopened for the purpose, including local services within Solihull where the S prefix was first used from 22 January 1966. Digbeth instead gathered in many of the bus services formerly operated by transferred garages but retained by Midland Red because they went out of the soon-to-be-created West Midlands county.

Digbeth was thus the last Midland Red bus garage in the Birmingham area. From 9 December 1978 it became a coach unit and all bus duties were transferred to garages

BELOW This is Benacre Street bus park with FEDD 2353 prominent in this August 1958 view. To the left is the rear of SON 2101 (DHA 719) which formed the office for the night security staff from 1955 to 1962, and was replaced by S10 3643. The latter was moved to Adderley Street yard when that took over. *F W York/ The Transport Museum, Wythall*

RIGHT The first bulk production of BMMO bodies permitted by the new Carlyle Works body shop was the 219 lightweight 'chassisless' S14 class which entered service in the mid-fifties, the culmination of development work with earlier chassisless experimental vehicles. They were neat looking but not as enjoyable to the ear as their immediate predecessors and, with single rear wheels as part of the weight savings, not particularly comfortable over a distance. Soon after entering service, 4671 was fitted with illuminated advertisement panels on each side. Like all single-deck buses in the fleet, 4671 had luggage racks so it was not possible to get the advertisement fluorescent tubes to illuminate the saloon too thus there was a separate set down the centre of the ceiling. The standard lighting on buses at the time was still filament bulbs. This is the Adderley Street yard used for overflow parking from the mid-1960s and which passed to the West Midlands PTE. *Ken Jubb*

BELOW RIGHT Another shot taken at Adderley Street yard on the same day in 1969. Midland Red purchased four Humber 4x4 recovery vehicles from the military and one is hauling a LS18 Leopard backwards, against a backdrop of D7s. *Ken Jubb*

LEFT The highly successful London motorway services warranted coaches to the revised permitted length of 36 feet to gain more seats. This led to the CM6T type, incorporating BMMO's 10.5 litre engine with semi-automatic gearbox, built in 1965-6 (see page 12 and 159). BMMO ceased vehicle production soon after and the next generation of motorway coaches were Leyland Leopards with Plaxton 44-seat coachwork including toilets. No 308 has just been delivered to Digbeth on trade plates on 30 March 1974 and will enter passenger service at the beginning of April. This is Mill Lane; the building line of Spencer House and the various garage exit doors behind the Leopard is interesting. *Garry Yates*

BELOW LEFT Midland Red took the opportunity to purchase small bits of land around Digbeth garage with a view to future expansion but, in the short term, once cleared of buildings they were available as boltholes for vehicle parking. A yard behind the garage was created on Mill Lane and used for parking vehicles from May 1958. 1949 S9 3372 was a Malvern bus en route to its home garage from works. It is thought that the conversion of the rear destination blind and number boxes to numbers only is unique to this bus. Hacking around its rear end did not end with this as it was converted to a tree cutter after withdrawal from bus services in 1963. A further purchase of land in 1973 extended Midland Red ownership as far as Bradford Street and vehicle maintenance shops were eventually built here, taking much of the pressure off the main coach loading area. *Ken Jubb*

TOP Some properties adjacent to the Rea Street entrance were purchased in 1958 and demolished ten years later when one final property was obtained, giving the opportunity to create another open parking area. Midland Red Express placed three MCW Metroliners into service in June 1984 numbered 566-8 (A666-8 XDA). No 567 was loaned to Shamrock & Rambler with additional luggage space in the lower saloon, the latter's 3113 (A113 KFX) coming to Express in exchange. 3113, 566 and 568 are seen on 1 August 1984 - the Metroliners were not happy here and very soon were exchanged for three Leyland Tiger/ Plaxton Paramounts with Eastern Counties, itself about to be split up – within weeks passing to the Ambassador Travel offshoot. The Metroliners thus had three operators in their first four months. *Malcolm Keeley*

TOP RIGHT Access was created between the new yard on Rea Street and the main body of the garage, visible behind 1064 (NOE 614R) and 1086 (BVP 776V), seen on 6 May 1990. These two Plaxton Supreme bodied Leyland Leopards had been new to Midland Red as 614 and 776. The stock of 1979-80 Leopards, including 776, was relegated for use on Midland Red West stage services in 1990-1. 614, new in 1976, had been upgraded in 1985, receiving a DAF engine and this modernised front. *Malcolm Keeley*

further afield apart from its share of the X12/112 which were deliberately retained until mopped up by the 'Lancer' MAP scheme on 17 February 1979. This transfer of bus services may seem rather surprising but Midland Red had the example of Coventry, successfully served for decades from outlying garages.

Apart from a few vehicles at Cannock and Leicester, all coaches were concentrated at Digbeth which also received the express services, tours, excursions and contracts of the Midland garages of National Travel (West), previously working out of the ex-Worthington Tours premises in Hurst Street, Birmingham, and ex-Don Everall in Bilston. Digbeth busmen now found themselves as coach drivers, a different job requiring different people skills, while senior men at other garages lost their premier coaching work. Some facelifting of the coach station was carried out over the years but it was blighted for many years by thoughts on a new location.

Upon the company split in 1981, the coaches passed to Midland Red Express which relaunched itself as Midland Red Coaches from 26 April 1985. A consortium of Midland Red West managers assumed responsibility for Midland Red Coaches upon bus service deregulation on 26 October 1986 and completed the buyout of both companies from the National Bus Company in December 1986. The Midland Red Coaches name was extended to Midland Red West coaches.

Deregulation day saw indigenous and secondhand Leyland Nationals of Midland Red West begin to run new routes plus socially desirable services in Birmingham and the Black Country not registered by West Midlands Travel, won under the tendering process operated by West Midlands Passenger Transport Executive. Midland Red West deployed Digbeth, the Bull Ring bus station and Carlyle Works at times in the operation and maintenance of the vehicles involved. Despite investment in new buses, Midland Red West and its First successor gradually retrenched from Birmingham and Black Country local services, and Digbeth concentrated on being Birmingham's coach station. After the years of blight, the coaches have stayed at Digbeth where an almost entire rebuild to the latest standards was completed in 2009.

ABOVE Midland Red purchased in 1976 some land on the opposite corner of Rea Street and used it for staff or coach parking, depending on season. One of the occupiers on 19 August 1981 was this ex-Harper Brothers Leyland Leopard 2251 (LRF 220K) with Plaxton front panel applied to its Duple body in 1980 after accident damage. *Malcolm Keeley*

BELOW A one-off in the fleet was this 1983 Leyland Royal Tiger B50 with Roe 50-seat body. Originally delivered in National Holidays livery to Midland Red (Express) as its no 555 (SOH 555Y), it had become 1009 in the Midland Red West fleet and gained this red livery when seen in the coach station on 30 June 1989. *Malcolm Keeley*

RIGHT In a trial run of the tendering procedure to apply generally after 26 October 1986, Midland Red Coaches won the Heart of England services between Solihull, Balsall Common and Coventry with effect from 16 June. Four 1982 Leyland Leopard/ Willowbrooks were fitted out for bus work in June 1986 and were joined by five ex-Fife Scottish 1971 Daimler Fleetlines with Alexander 75-seat bodies – lower height versions of the Fleetlines familiarly operated by Midland Red. The nine vehicles ran until deregulation in October 1986. Fleetline 59 (RXA 59J) is seen in Blossomfield Road, Solihull, on 1 July 1986. *Malcolm Keeley*

BIRMINGHAM SHEEPCOTE STREET

Opened: 19 August 1951
To West Midlands Passenger Transport Executive 3 December 1973
Closed: 15 November 1975

This garage with red brick frontage was acquired from British Road Services and thus lacked the BMMO style. It had a roof of wooden 'Belfast' construction rather than the usual steel. It could cater for 70 vehicles, 40 under cover, relieving the need to park buses on the land fronting Digbeth required for road widening. Sheepcote Street shared the DH code with Digbeth until its buses received new blinds with the SH code in 1961. Its vehicles were predominantly double-deck buses plus a coach. BMMO types were accompanied by Daimlers, firstly the wartime buses drafted in upon opening from Digbeth and, later, Fleetlines in some force. In addition to a share in the Walsall Road services, transferred to Birmingham City Transport in 1957-8, and assisting the Stratford Road routes, the garage particularly worked services to the east of the city via the Coleshill Road. This later

Two wartime Daimler CWA6 buses after modernisation in 1950-1 stand in the doorways of Sheepcote Street garage. *BMMO*

included Chelmsley Wood, the large estate developed from 1967 onwards and always served by driver only buses.

Sheepcote Street and the ex-BCT garage at Moseley Road, reopened to work services received by the PTE formerly operated by Digbeth, were closed upon the first major network changes after the takeover. One of the consequences was the transfer of BMMO single-deck buses to unlikely homes, the ex-Birmingham City Transport garages Coventry Road, Lea Hall and Yardley Wood.

BANBURY

Opened: 13 October 1919

To Midland Red South 6 September 1981. To Stagecoach December 1993

Still in use

Similar to other country towns, the original BMMO operation at Banbury comprised three vehicles, the minimum of manpower and a supply of handbills to post through letterboxes, advising that Midland Red buses would begin running the following day – to the disgust of proprietors of horse-drawn carrier carts plying to and from the towns, particularly on market days. The 1928 service renumbering allocated 479-512 to Banbury but they did eventually creep up to 516.

The company's first premises on Canal Street were originally leased but subsequently purchased along with adjoining land where a new garage was opened on 25 September 1931. The first premises were then resold to the original owner. The new steel framed garage had brick-built offices and workshops. Its capacity of 18 buses was inadequate by the 1940s but fortunately there was generous land to the rear, enabling an extension with a side entrance. Post-war building restrictions delayed matters, the extension not opening until late 1952 after which 50 vehicles could be accommodated.

The company circulated its accident records around the garages and Banbury's relatively tranquil local and rural services always did well, especially compared to Birmingham buses which operated through the cut and thrust of city traffic. The B prefix for local services was first used on 10 July 1933. Country services ran to some relatively distant places including Buckingham, Coventry, Leamington, Northampton and Rugby. Pre-war Traffic Manager O C Power was not keen on the rather detached Banbury operations and, many years later, the Stagecoach decision to place them with its Oxford subsidiary matched his line of thought.

Non-BMMO types familiar at Banbury included AD2s and LS18s. The local identity name 'Ridercross', introduced with a local network revision in July 1981, delightfully recalled the nursery rhyme associated with the famous Banbury Cross in the middle of the town but Midland Red South abandoned such names in 1983.

Some Bedfords and Leopards of Tanners International of Sibford Gower were taken over on 4 September 1989, the company having latterly been a competitor on Banbury town services.

Staff had to work from the original garage for a time without the benefit of a roof but one had been fitted by this July 1927 view.
The Transport Museum, Wythall collection

31

ABOVE Early days at Banbury with OB 1106, a Tilling-Stevens TS3 dating from 1916. *MRK collection*

LEFT The later garage as it looked in 1960, showing the side access to the 1952 extension. The original garage is at the far end. *Paul Gray*

BELOW The interior of Banbury garage shortly after the extension built in 1952. The section of cladding up to the ridge immediately behind S13 3947, SON 2048 and S10 3718 marks the original back wall of the garage. All the space behind the buses comprised the extension which was wider than the original building and additionally accessed by the side exit. *MRK collection*

ABOVE Banbury Bus Station opened in 1965 and D7 4431 is seen there working a local service four years later. *Ken Jubb*

LEFT Canal Street on 16 November 1994 showing both the original garage and the one that has now been in use for over eighty years. *Garry Yates*

BELOW 1976 Leyland National 506 still carries the Ridercross branding on 18 September 1984. *Malcolm Keeley*

BROMSGROVE

Opened: 26 July 1920

To Midland Red West 6 September 1981

Closed: 16 September 1983

The garage on The Strand, Birmingham Road, was an early example of Midland Red's evolving architectural style, being a steel frame building with a frontage of red brick with stone facings. An extension to the rear brought into operation in December 1930 increased its capacity from 24 to 47. The Ministry of Aircraft Production requisitioned a large part of the garage during World War Two to enable Austin to manufacture large aero components such as 'Spitfire' wings and 'Stirling' bomber parts. The vehicle capacity was exceeded in the years immediately after World War Two but a further extension, opened on 1 February 1956, allowed up to 65 of the slightly larger buses of the time.

Bromsgrove garage had a share in the important 144 service, other routes to Birmingham were the 143 and 145 via Lickey and West Heath respectively. Other Bromsgrove-worked routes included those to Redditch, Kidderminster, Stourbridge, Droitwich and Stratford-upon-Avon. The 1928 service renumbering allocated 318-351 to Bromsgrove and Redditch. Use of the B prefix for a handful of local services began on 1 September 1952. There were also A-prefixed works services to Austin (later British Leyland) at Longbridge that, at certain times, could engage half the Bromsgrove allocation. The 144 was among those to receive the first double-deck buses with platform doors, the D5Bs, but the heavy buses proved unable to work all day without refuelling. Fortunately the company maintained premises to assist the many services operating from Station Street, Birmingham. Its yard included a refuelling facility providing a temporary solution but the garages were early recipients of lightweight D7s that took over most 144 duties.

BELOW The unrelieved red livery was introduced in 1956 and a single early example in the form of D7 4115 helps to date this interior view of Bromsgrove garage. Another D7, 4107, sits among several early post-war single-deckers but on the right is SON 2428 - a FEDD is just visible beyond. *BMMO*

RIGHT This view shows the garage available for disposal in the autumn of 1971. The garage was first closed on the last day of that year and its duties distributed widely. It was sold and repurchased for re-opening on 3 December 1973 to take on Worcestershire work from garages passed to West Midlands PTE. Soon afterwards the tenancy on the Enquiry Office in the town was not renewed, the business being transferred to the garage in June 1976. The garage was closed in 1983, most work then passing to Kidderminster and Worcester, and used for storage until demolition in 1987. *Ken Jubb*

BELOW RIGHT The 144 service originally took around three hours to travel from Birmingham through Rubery, Bromsgrove and Worcester to the Malverns but improved buses allowed timings to be speeded up from 12 January 1929. It then took 2 hours 20 minutes each way, a timing that lasted for decades. The service was very successful and double-deck buses would run every 20 minutes, increased to a 15-minute headway on Saturdays with massive duplication on bank holidays. 2236 was a Worcester FEDD although loaned to Bromsgrove from time to time – wherever it was working from, Bromsgrove garage's facilities attracted the attention of its conductress in May 1957 by which time the 144 was generally worked by D7s or Digbeth's LD8s. The FEDDs were light and, if well maintained, could keep up with D7s and LD8s while AD2s and D5s could not. *F W York/ The Transport Museum, Wythall*

RIGHT The LRR service coaches and OLR touring vehicles were relegated to bus services during World War Two and never reverted to coaches. The LRRs were upseated from 30 to 34 and became particularly associated with Leamington garage. No 1644, new in 1935, however moved to Bromsgrove in 1950 and is thought here to be parked on Recreation Road car park. *Mike Rooum*

BELOW RIGHT Numerically the first production post-war BMMO, S6 class 3000, is parked at Stratford just before its retirement in August 1964. It will be returning to Bromsgrove on the 338 via Hanbury and Droitwich. Passenger Transport Journal sang the praises of this bus in November 1946, noting that three hundred were to be produced – in the event two hundred were S8 and S9 models built six inches wider to the newly permitted width of eight feet but the S6 was the beginning of an iconic series of buses. The magazine described the centre underfloor-engined vehicle as 'a landmark in the history of British design and operation of public service vehicles …. with the adoption of a chassis of unconventional design in association with a body which may, at last, be described as fully all-metal'. All the early post-war single-decker service buses were lengthened from 27 feet 6 inches to 29 feet 3 inches between 1951 and 1953 following a relaxation in permitted dimensions. This allowed an extra row of seats, increasing capacity from 40 to 44. Fortunately they had their back axles relatively far back so the rear overhang did not become excessive. The 338 was a once-a-week summer only service that did not run after 1964; the marginally more significant route to Bromsgrove was the 339 via Alcester and Redditch. *Ken Jubb*

RIGHT The first attempt at Droitwich local services began on 29 November 1958 and lasted seven months. Midland Red had another bash from 26 October 1968, following the considerable amount of new housing in the town, with the D50/51, followed by the D52/53 from 14 February 1970. Bromsgrove supplied buses, both S17s seen here, 5491 and 5709, belonging to the garage. All four routes last ran on 3 April 1971 and were taken on by Everton Coaches Ltd. *Ken Jubb*

CANNOCK

Opened: 7 February 1977

To Midland Red North 6 September 1981, relaunched as Arriva 1997

Still in use

The ex-Harper Brothers garage at Heath Hayes was replaced by new premises at Delta Way, Cannock which also took on services in the Wolverhampton area operated by Cradley Heath since the WMPTE agreement in December 1973. The opening allocation of 78 buses immediately ranked it the largest on the system, staffed by an interesting mix of Midland Red Black Country and ex-Harpers personnel!

The garage shared the 'Chaserider' branding with Stafford. The complexities of the changes meant 'Chaserider' was introduced in two stages and the new network in the Cannock area commenced on 31 August 1980. Certain routes were exchanged with West Midlands PTE for operational convenience and to maintain the existing balance of revenue, although both operators achieved significant savings. The maroon 'Chaserider' branding stripe was created by mixing Midland Red with the blue of West Midlands PTE.

Cannock was the headquarters of Midland Red (North) after the 1981 split. Midland Red (Express) initially outstationed some coaches at Cannock for contract and express operations but this work was transferred to Midland Red (North) from 16 October 1982. Ford Transit minibuses were launched at Cannock with free rides on 28 June 1986 and normal services from two days later.

ABOVE Cannock garage when new with two Nationals, a Leopard coach and one of the two ECW-bodied Daimler Fleetlines ordered by Harper Brothers but delivered to Midland Red. *MROC*

BELOW MAN articulated buses, comprising a 1978 prototype and four 1979 vehicles, were operated from new by South Yorkshire PTE. After the PTE experiment was over, the five were hired from MAN-VW Truck & Bus by City of Oxford and then entered the orbit of the ex-Midland Red companies when Express borrowed them for Park and Ride services at the 1982 Motor Show, held at the National Exhibition Centre in Solihull. West had them on loan throughout 1983 for work at Redditch; they were purchased by North at the beginning of 1984 and numbered 1801-5. Seating 53, they began falling out of use before deregulation in October 1986, although 1801/4 were relicensed for hire to the short-lived Solihull District bus company. All ceased work by the end of February 1987 and they were sold to an Australian company. 1802 is seen in Cannock on 27 July 1985, loading in the town while the bus station was being rebuilt. Unlike the others, Midland Red North preferred to trade under the local identity names introduced with the Market Analysis Project. *Malcolm Keeley*

COALVILLE

Opened: 6 December 1925
To Midland Red East 6 September 1981; relaunched as Midland Fox January 1984, relaunched as Arriva 1997
Closed: 26 March 2011

The town's name is highly descriptive and the winding wheel of the colliery immediately to the rear overlooked the bus garage on Ashby Road. The latter was constructed in classic BMMO architectural style of the period and was soon extended in 1930 and again in 1938, by which time it could hold 75 vehicles. Steel-framed with brick constructed offices and workshops, it included a Booking and Enquiry Office on the frontage. Land purchases by BMMO included a row of cottages, the nearest one being used as a store by the company for many years. The portion of the garage to the rear of the cottages was requisitioned during World War Two to store heavy machinery and other equipment.

Non-BMMO classes to be found at Coalville included AD2 and LS18 types. The town was not served by any of the well-known glamour routes but the garage did have some 'quality' work in the form of a share in the X99 Birmingham – Nottingham service. This meant dual-purpose single-deckers on the allocation. As may be implied by the town's name, there were a number of colliery services. Otherwise it was a mix of local and inter-suburban services, especially to Leicester, operating from there to Ibstock, Heather, Ashby and Burton, Kirby Muxloe and Bagworth. Other places reached by Coalville garage buses included Loughborough, Melbourne via Worthington, and Hinckley via Market Bosworth.

The C prefix was first used for local services on the last day of 1938 but subsequently disappeared. Some MAP schemes meant the end of prefix letters but the 'Lancer' network introduced on 17 February 1979 brought them back to Coalville, albeit with different

ABOVE A very early view of Coalville garage with a char-a-banc just visible inside. Note there were originally only two doorways on the frontage. *The Transport Museum, Wythall collection*

ABOVE RIGHT This piece of land, approximately 100 metres from the garage, was used for parking vehicles between work. The S9 class consisted of 100 buses bodied by Brush, delivered in 1949-50. Half featured rear destination blinds, provided on all vehicles since World War Two, but provision was reduced to numbers only on the second half, commencing with 3407. Nos 3383 and 3420 provide a useful comparison in 1960. The C77 Whitwick Circular was replaced by a revised and extended C90 in 1967 although the C77 identification was retained for a time for schools journeys. *Ken Jubb*

RIGHT There were a hundred S8s, new in 1948-9, all bodied by Metro-Cammell. Three were fitted with S15 fronts and improved interiors in 1957-8, including 3241 here which spent some time at Coalville and has just worked the 676 from Loughborough via Belton. *Ken Jubb*

numbers (C1-7). The 'Lancer' name, shared with Swadlincote, was chosen because of local connections with Ivanhoe.

After the split, Midland Red East's Coalville garage and Midland Red North from Tamworth ran the X99 jointly as a Midland Express service. 'Lancer' was the only local identity name in the Midland Red East area, the new company ridding itself of it at the earliest opportunity when services were revised and renumbered in the 1xx series from 27 February 1982. The first 'Fox Cub' minibuses were introduced here on 27 July 1985.

RIGHT Coalville garage on 17 August 1985 is host to 3830, a Leyland National 2 that in 1980 was almost the last bus delivered to the old Midland Red. Under Midland Fox it has received a wheelchair lift, Midland Express livery and glamorous wheeltrims. *Malcolm Keeley*

BELOW The main road frontage had three doors once the 1930 extension was completed. Midland Red subsequently blocked up two and windows were provided instead as seen on 18 May 1996. *Garry Yates*

COVENTRY

Opened: 1 March 1921
Closed: 29 September 1923

The company leased premises to the rear of 33 Sandy Lane with room for around half a dozen buses. Other than this sojourn, BMMO managed without any garage in this important city. Coventry ran its own public transport network, absorbed into West Midlands PTE on 1 April 1974, so Midland Red had no local services here. Operating centres were developed in nearby towns instead. Digbeth garage ran the services to Birmingham, Nuneaton and Hinckley covered the north, Rugby served the east and Leamington the south. This was perhaps fortunate

because the city centre, previously very attractive, was devastated in a World War Two air raid on 14 November 1940, among other things rendering the city's tramway system unworkable. Midland Red was lucky in terms of property destruction during World War Two but its Coventry services and works journeys were daily put under tremendous strain by the movement of people to areas considered safer outside the city, returning the next morning.

Although not a Midland Red property, it is worth mentioning Pool Meadow Bus Station which opened on 26 October 1931.

CRADLEY HEATH

Opened: 27 March 1939
Closed: 6 February 1977

The town is on the southern fringe of the Black Country industrial belt and became famous for its chain-making, a speciality among its iron smelting, forging and engineering industries. Midland Red was involved with two premises in the town before opening its own garage in 1939.

A leased wooden garage in King Street (nowadays called Prince Street to avoid confusion with King Street in nearby Old Hill) was taken over on 24 May 1930 with the Great Western Railway's vehicles for its Cradley Heath – Dudley service which was subsumed into BMMO's existing 243, operated by Dudley garage. The King Street premises were thus redundant and, after BMMO struggled to find and then lost the first tenant, negotiations to surrender the lease were completed on 14 April 1932.

Midland Red leased part of a Great Western Railway goods shed accessed from Corngreaves Road, Cradley Heath, from 13 April 1936. It was simply a galvanized iron shed with steel doors at each end. BMMO concreted the floor and installed various fittings including an underground petrol tank later utilized at Oldbury. 11 vehicles were housed there from 25 May 1936 with engineering staff which, at that time, included the drivers. Conductors booked on at Stourbridge and returned there to pay in, the dead time incurred being cheaper than having inspectors and cash clerks at Cradley. The last day of operation was 30 September 1936.

A purpose-built garage was opened in Forge Lane, opposite the railway station, including a Booking and Enquiry Office on the red brick frontage. The undercover area was capable of holding 70 buses but never actually reached that number. Opened in 1939, just six months before the outbreak of World War Two, it was the only garage to be provided with an Air Raid Shelter as a permanent feature, to meet regulations then in force.

In 1946 it was the first garage to become a centralised dock for overhauling vehicles, serving the western area garages after the opening of Leicester Wigston. Various single-deck prototypes and experimental vehicles ran from here in the 1950s including the solitary LA 3977 and S12s with trial AEC, Leyland and BMMO engines from mid-1951. The first thirty-footer, prototype S13 3694, was a familiar sight for many years. Non-BMMO types included AD2 AEC Regents. The garage code changed from CY to CH in 1968.

The garage was one of several serving the Black Country towns. It ran locals in the Cradley Heath, Old Hill and Blackheath vicinities, other destinations included Birmingham, Dudley, Wednesbury, Stourbridge, Gornal,

A view of the garage in 1971 *Ken Jubb*

Halesowen and Romsley. The August 1947 Staff Bulletin includes Stourbridge locals S37/38 to Wynall among Cradley Heath's work. Peter Carpenter's book on the garage reveals the degree its available space was used to take on services as demand grew in neighbouring townships – including work on Dudley's D-prefix locals and Brierley Hill's B39.

It was closed on 28 May in the 1971 economies but reopened in December 1973 to operate Midland Red services previously worked by garages passed to WMPTE, or taken over from WMPTE in the Wolverhampton area. This was a temporary arrangement until a new garage in Cannock was opened. The building still exists at the time of writing.

RIGHT The Booking and Enquiry Office located on the garage frontage. *BMMO*

BELOW Early post-war Interior view of Cradley Heath with modern buses marshalled for the official photographer – S8 3243, S6 3073, S8 3226, and AD2s 3111 and 3108. The buses behind are all pre-war. *BMMO*

ABOVE 1936 FEDD/ Metro-Cammell 1752 (BHA 310) has terminated at Cradley Heath station - a hop, skip and a jump away from the garage. *MRK collection*

RIGHT The Brush body of 1939 SON 2313 had this experimental styling and was replaced by the standard Nudd-rebuilt body off 2325, withdrawn in 1954. 2313 spent most of its post-war career with original body at Cradley Heath but did also work in that condition from Stourbridge and Kidderminster. It was finally retired in 1958. *MRK collection*

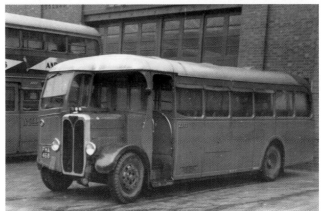

BELOW Midland Red's first 36-feet long bus, S16 5095, entered service at Cradley Heath during Easter 1962 after a period of tests. A moving contrast to this triumph is the very last BMMO bus of all, S23 5991, looking immaculate upon being placed on the road at the same garage in June 1970. This is Dudley Bus Station. *Ken Jubb*

DUDLEY

Opened: 2 August 1929

To West Midlands Passenger Transport Executive 3 December 1973; to West Midlands Travel 26 October 1986

Closed: 28 August 1993

The ancient borough of Dudley was, for many years, an island of Worcestershire surrounded by the southern tip of Staffordshire, rather like its ruined hilltop castle that also became surrounded on its wooded slopes by an open-air zoo that for many years generated huge demands on high days and holidays for Midland Red buses. Dudley's heritage is also industrial, however, being an area rich in deposits of coal and iron ore.

Midland Red was brought in during 1924 to deal with opposition buses competing with the BET-owned tramways and then they replaced the trams themselves. The addition of other routes meant a dense Midland Red network rapidly developed.

The garage for 50 vehicles was in Birmingham Road and included a Booking and Enquiry Office within a traditional BMMO steel frame red brick design. A large area of land was later acquired and used to park vehicles. Subsidence caused by old mines beneath the property sometimes caused problems.

In addition to reaching Birmingham via various routes, there were services from Wednesbury running across the town to Cradley and Stourbridge. Many of the local services, for which D prefix letters were introduced on 1 October 1934, were very challenging in terms of gradient and road surfaces. Journeys to Kingswinford and Wall Heath were a breath of

BELOW Dudley garage in the 1950s with a C1 just inside the doorway. The double-deck buses passing outside are a West Bromwich Corporation Daimler COG6 on the 74 and a Midland Red FEDD on the B87 – both new as tramway replacements in 1939. *BMMO*

RIGHT The area is legendary for its hills; City Road being arguably the worst of some notable climbs. This demanding territory was for many years accompanied by poor road surfaces exacerbated by the weather, with nothing higher to the east before the Urals! The bus station was, unhelpfully, located on a steep grade and there was the occasional runaway bus with tragic results. The Meadows 6DC 10.35 litre engines of the twenty 1949 GD6 Guy Arabs provided ample power but had awkwardly placed ancillaries when fitted to a bus rather than a truck. This increased servicing and repair times so they were replaced in 1952 by BMMO 8 litre units. Guy also built the 56-seat bodies, employing Park Royal frames. The GD6s may have had plenty of power, even after the engine changes, and much better driver visibility but there is no denying they looked old compared to the contemporary D5s. Land on the opposite side of Birmingham Road was available for buses not immediately required for service and four GD6s are seen here – 3575, nearest to the camera, has had its front upper deck windows replaced. The GD6s were taken out of service between November 1961 and December 1962. Dudley's allocation also surprisingly included some of the AD2 AEC Regents, despite their poor power-to-weight ratio in such challenging terrain. *Ken Jubb*

BELOW RIGHT Two D5Bs led by 3844 await their next duties at Dudley garage. 3844 was new in 1951 and had a fifteen-year life. *Maurice Collignon*

fresh air. Dudley's operations also included contributing to the long 865 service from the town to Stafford. The route went via Walsall and was jointly worked with Walsall Corporation which was absorbed into West Midlands Passenger Transport Executive in 1969. The municipal operators ran a few services into Dudley, including Wolverhampton's trolleybuses, but Midland Red basically ruled the roost. Double-deck buses formed the majority of the allocation from the mid-1930s although the BRR single-deckers were familiar here too. The power-to-weight ratio of the 1949 GD6 class Guys was very welcome on Dudley's hills.

The transfer to West Midlands PTE in December 1973 arguably had the greatest impact here. Only the X96 family of long-distance services survived and even they were soon re-routed, ending Midland Red's huge association with the town. The garage has now gone, the site being part of a large traffic gyratory.

TOP 1962 S15 5085 provided comfortable rides from Dudley for many years although, by the time of this 1971 shot, it had been downgraded from dual-purpose to bus status. *Ken Jubb*

ABOVE D12 Fleetline 6136 manoeuvres through fumes created by S17 5594, ticking over in Dudley garage on 11 November 1973. The S17 passed to WMPTE a month later but the Fleetline remained with Midland Red, working services from Cradley Heath garage. *Garry Yates*

EVESHAM

Opened: 25 August 1931
To Midland Red West 6 September 1981, relaunched as First November 2001
Closed: 31 December 2006

The garage in this market town, surrounded by orchards and farmlands, had arguably the most rural territory on the system although Evesham itself in summertime took on the feel of an inland holiday resort. The garage on Abbey Road was originally a single bay steel framed corrugated iron structure capable of holding 16 buses, with timber framed offices. Additional land adjoining the garage was purchased, enabling the garage to be extended and modernised in the mid-1950s to become a virtually new garage in the classic BMMO post–World War Two style. It could then hold 28 buses with a further substantial area for outdoor parking.

Evesham's main claim to fame (or infamy) for its vehicle stock came in World War Two when the entire allocation was converted to run on producer gas. Double-deck buses were included in the allocation from the mid-1940s. The AD2 class was represented but more significant were five consecutive D5Bs, the first class with platform doors, 3809-13 being originally allocated to the long 148 service to Birmingham.

Services around Evesham and Pershore were numbered between 381 and 408. The E prefix was introduced for local services on 2 February 1946. It must have been delightful to work

Evesham's allocation of double-deck buses were kept occupied on the 148 to Birmingham and, when their initial glory days were over, on the 394/5 to Offenham, and the 389 to popular Broadway and that secret gem just down the road, Willersey, where D5B 3812 will visit next. Terminating buses would gather here on the High Street. Changing the destinations on post-war half-cab double-deckers was somewhat undignified, with the left foot flailing about, especially for shorter personnel. *Andrew Willis*

here, except when it snowed or the River Avon was in flood! The garage covered services around and beyond the beautiful Vale of Evesham. This included routes to Chipping Campden and onwards to Moreton-in-Marsh (392) and Stratford-upon-Avon (524), in the other direction buses ran to Pershore and Worcester. Among the villages served between Evesham and Pershore was Bricklehampton, unbeaten as the longest name in England without repeating a letter of the alphabet.

The MAP-derived 'Wayfarer' network was introduced on 23 July 1977. All services in the new network were numbered in a series previously associated with Midland Red's Black Country operations, now with West Midlands PTE, and the E prefix departed. The 'Wayfarer' name was discontinued from July 1984.

A new bus parking area at Redditch in 1978 meant the end of five Evesham-based buses being used on Redditch local services, reducing the Evesham allocation to only twelve. The garage was modified, allowing around half the building and most of the outside parking area to be sold to the Milk Marketing Board on 19 March 1980. Low passenger revenues meant Evesham in later years received older buses in the fleet but, in 2005, the garage received some Alexander Dennis Enviro 300s – the first new buses since National 773 was delivered in January 1980. The end was near, however, and the garage was closed as First gave up many Worcestershire County Council funded contracts and schools services. Demolition followed soon after.

RIGHT Midland Red could offer candidates for the longest and shortest stage carriage services in England. The delightful town of Pershore with its fine Georgian houses was particularly blessed in this regard. The X91 between Hereford and Leicester via Pershore took five and a half hours to wend from end to end, around 10 minutes longer than the better known X96 between Shrewsbury and Northampton. Meanwhile Pershore's 'local' railway station was some distance out of the town and the Great Western Railway's linking services between Pershore, the station and to Wyre Piddle passed to Midland Red on 15 February 1932. The successor 383 was a candidate for the company's shortest journeys although at times they were extended to the nearby RAF station, Pinvin or across town to the Abbey Estate. S14 4349 is seen loading in the centre of Pershore - this had been the prototype one-man operated bus, as it would have been described at the time of its entry into service in 1956 at Hereford. The cab was fully enclosed and entered at the rear to protect the driver and the company's money, a degree of security soon thought unnecessary. The cab was elongated, originally to accommodate a Brandt change machine - this and a parcels box on the nearside reduced seating capacity from 44 to 40. *Ken Jubb*

BELOW LEFT Not many garages belonging to big operators had such an uplifting view from the doorway as Evesham. S6 3098 is on the roadway outside in 1963 with a not very helpful via display. Evesham did not generate anywhere near this number of local services but the E3 to Fairfield estate was extended from 7 October 1961 to Barnard Close as E3 or via Battleton Road as E13. *Ken Jubb*

BELOW Midland Red had a Horticultural Society which held an Annual Show. With crops literally up to the garage boundary, Evesham kindly did not compete but always sent a superb display. S17 5699 is ex-works in late 1968, the cautionary sticker advising against machine washing is in the driver's signalling window. *Ken Jubb*

RIGHT A superb journey is in prospect for those at Stratford-upon-Avon boarding 1969 DD13 Daimler Fleetline/ Alexander 6221, still looking very smart in 1970, and the front seats are already taken. Stratford Blue operated the direct services to Evesham via Bidford, taking around an hour. Midland Red's infrequent but highly scenic 524 wandered via Mickleton, Chipping Campden, down the enchanting hill to Aston-sub-Edge, Weston-sub-Edge, Willersey and Broadway, taking around half an hour longer to reach Evesham. *Ken Jubb*

LEFT Midland Red shortened a number of Plaxton-bodied 45-seat Fords to 27-seaters from 1977 as a possible alternative to van-based minibuses. This work was carried out at Carlyle Works, where innovation clearly was not dead, and some were sold to other NBC companies. No 370, new in 1974, was seen at Evesham on 7 November 1981. *Malcolm Keeley*

BELOW Midland Red West obtained two Bedford coaches from Yeomans of Canon Pyon, initially to assist with competition in Hereford on the ex-Yeomans service to Credenhill. The Bedfords were released from bus work by ex-Northern General Leyland Nationals in May 1984 and became part of the coach fleet. Being serviced at Evesham on 7 August 1984 is 845 (NVJ 600R), an ex-Yeomans 1976 Bedford YMT with Duple 'Dominant Express' 53-seat coachwork and 175 (OCN 775M), a 1973 National ex-Northern. *Malcolm Keeley*

RIGHT One of the fifty Leyland Lynx buses with Cummins engines purchased by Midland Red West in 1990 passes through Chipping Campden on 24 April 2002. No 1149 retains MRW livery but First branding is now carried. *Malcolm Keeley*

ABOVE While Midland Red West kept the aura of the big company operator about it, placing large orders for new buses, it also adopted the very traditional approach of using depreciated relegated coaches to cover low revenue rural services. Midland Red West received six of these Plaxton-bodied Leyland Tigers in 1985 but 1003 was bus-liveried and operating a local to Evesham in Offenham on 24 April 2002. The MRW livery (modified with First fleetnames) was both traditional and modern, not fighting with the lines of their vehicles. The replacing First 'Barbie' corporate colours are either loved or hated but had a tough act to follow here. 1003 lasted long enough to receive fleet number 22003 when five digit fleet numbers covering First's entire UK operations were introduced in 2004. *Malcolm Keeley*

HALESOWEN

Opened: 24 May 1930

Closed: 31 October 1930

Space was rented from J B Downing in New Road for three buses, continuing an arrangement inherited from the Great Western Railway. The buses operated a service between Halesowen and Old Hill station that had replaced GWR passenger trains in 1927. The service was numbered 229 by BMMO and in July SOS buses replaced the three ex-GWR Maudslays which were transferred briefly to Hereford. The 229 was operated by Dudley garage after closure.

HARTSHILL

Opened: 27 May 1925

To West Midlands Passenger Transport Executive 3 December 1973; to West Midlands Travel 26 October 1986

Closed: 2 October 1993

To the north of Brierley Hill, the town that grew famous for its iron and steelworks, glassware and firebricks, was Hartshill depot, on Dudley Road in Hart's Hill. Midland Red insisted on spelling it as Hartshill, leading to many a query! The depot was built for electric tramcars around 1899 but, as the fortunes of the Black Country tramways started to wane, the trams ceased to use this depot after 28 February 1925 and it was acquired by BMMO. What was originally the tramway manager's house became the Booking and Enquiry Office. The largely brick garage buildings were extended in 1931 with an additional bay over what had been the entrance to the tram sheds, increasing the capacity to 58 vehicles.

A major rebuild completed in late 1964 disguised much of the tramway origins. A detached two-storey brick building containing the Traffic office block and canteen was built on the frontage alongside the existing garage. A new lean-to

Engineering office block with shops and stores was provided adjacent to the main bay. A rear entrance was added to the garage with a refuelling bay to improve the flow of vehicles. The old Traffic and Engineering offices were demolished and today the rest has met the same fate.

When the garage opened, its allocation entirely comprised new Standard SOS buses. Double-deck buses gradually took over most of the allocation. The 1942 AEC Regents built for Coventry ran from here from 1949, alongside a few mechanically similar AD2s. There were a lot of D5s here and a few LD8s.

The garage's biggest responsibility was the 245/6 (Stourbridge-Dudley-Wednesbury) which, in early post-war years, required around 25 buses, 21 being supplied by Hartshill. Work was almost entirely confined to the Black Country, also connecting Brierley Hill to townships such as Old Hill, Cradley Heath, Blackheath, Halesowen, Pensnett, Gornal Wood and Kingswinford – some services operating through to Birmingham. There was considerable overlap with Dudley's operations – for many years Hartshill was a major contributor to the 140 Dudley to Birmingham service - but let's not forget Brierley Hill's local service. The B39 to Upper Pensnett estate was a late and lonely entrant to the list of prefixed bus services introduced on 4 November 1963.

LEFT Interior of the depot in July 1927. *The Transport Museum, Wythall collection*

TOP This view shows the Booking and Enquiry Office in the office block on the frontage, dressed for the Coronation of Queen Elizabeth II in 1953. The 1931 extension is on the left, not entirely hiding the gable ends of the original tramway sheds. *BMMO*

ABOVE RIGHT A closer view of the booking office. *BMMO*

RIGHT 2442 was one of six AEC Regents (2441-6) originally built in 1942 for Coventry Corporation but diverted to Midland Red. It is seen at Stourbridge after the Brush body had been extensively rebuilt in 1951 at Hooton with flush glazing and sliding ventilators, post-war destination indicators, and the unusual built-up front wings. The six Regents were withdrawn in 1954-5. *Gordon Davies*

RIGHT The garage provided vehicles for the D17 from Dudley Bus Station, seen here, to Woodside, not far from Harts Hill. D5 3497 operated from Hartshill garage for its entire life from 1949 to 1963. This particular vehicle is interesting because the main side windows of its Brush body are flush mounted in rubber, a style of glazing not favoured on BMMO designed bodies until the S23 although much favoured elsewhere from the 1950s. *Alan D Broughall*

BELOW RIGHT The concept of underfloor-engine double-deck buses was mentioned in the staff magazine as far back as 1949 but it was another decade before they became reality. When new in 1960, the first D10 received an ecstatic response in the trade press; the Motor Transport reporter describing Midland Red as the 'bus operating company which has so often pointed the way for the makers' designers to follow' although, in this case, the manufacturers did not follow!

4943 had a single entrance at the front but buses of this layout were known to suffer a pinch point at the foot of the stairs, making them slower to load. A two-door, twin staircase arrangement, seating only 65, was therefore tested on the second D10, 4944, with alighting passengers directed to use the rear. The two D10 layouts were tested in service alongside D9s working from Hartshill garage, this lucky shot capturing both at Dudley bus station while working the 246 to Stourbridge. The loss of seats on 4944 was not worthwhile and it was rebuilt to single door and staircase in November 1962. The D10 was not unsuccessful but its advantage over the simpler D9 for one-man operation could not have been foreseen at the time. *Ken Jubb*

RIGHT The garage just after the WMPTE takeover and 1963 D11 Fleetline 5256 has WM vinyls added. *Ken Jubb*

HEATH HAYES

Taken over from Harper Brothers with effect from 22 April 1974

Closed: 6 February 1977

The largest independent bus operator in Staffordshire, Harper Brothers of Heath Hayes, was taken over in 1974, the deal also including the Heath Hayes garage. The takeover was somewhat protracted, the purchase being agreed on 21 March. The Traffic Commissioners granted short-term licences on 22 April on which date the property and vehicles passed into Midland Red ownership – the vehicles gaining 'On hire to Midland Red' labels. The public date of transfer was 7 September when the legal lettering changed on the vehicles and Midland Red service numbers were adopted. Heath Hayes was replaced by new premises at Delta Way, Cannock.

BELOW Harper 31 (the future 2231) at Cannock Bus Station is already carrying a Midland Red identification in the windscreen in the spring of 1974. Harpers had regularly bought pairs of double-deckers since commencing its Birmingham service in 1965. This was one of two Northern Counties-bodied Daimler Fleetlines new in July 1971; a similar pair had been received in May 1970. *David Barber*

ABOVE Harper Brothers had two ECW-bodied Daimler Fleetlines on order at the time of takeover. They were delivered direct to Midland Red in 1976 and were the last new double-deck buses placed in service by the company which gave them the classification D14. Nos 439 and 440 are seen in the garage exit to Hednesford Road immediately after delivery; they were sold in Midland Red North's big cuts of April 1987. *Paul Roberts*

ABOVE LEFT 1973 Midland Red Leopard/ Marshall 221 was an appealing addition to the garage stock and is seen parked over the running pit. Behind, still in Harpers' colours, is TRE 949L, a 1973 Daimler Fleetline with Leyland O680 engine and ECW body that would receive the number 2234. Double-deckers had to take this route through the garage as the way to the left was not high enough. *Paul Roberts*

LEFT Midland Red only had ten of these Leopards with long-windowed Willowbrook bodies, regarded as semi-coaches when delivered in 1967 as the LS20 class. They had a rarity value anywhere on the system so the arrival of 5841 at Heath Hayes in 1976 was doubly interesting. Buses usually exited the garage via Hednesford Road, this door to Cannock Road mostly being used as an entrance. 5841, however, has come off one of the maintenance pits at this end of the garage and the driver is sorting out the destination etc before setting off on contract service C20. *Paul Roberts*

ABOVE 2146 was a 1971 Bedford YRQ with Duple 'Viceroy' 54-seat coachwork acquired with the fleet of Cooper, Oakengates, in October 1973. Originally allocated to Wellington, it was stored from September 1974 but the management evidently thought, being a Bedford, it could be inflicted on the ex-Harper employees at Heath Hayes where it re-entered service in August 1975! Midland Red gave the number 818 to Harpers' Lichfield – Aldridge – Kingstanding service. Some former Green Bus routes were transferred in March 1976 from Tamworth to Heath Hayes. It was therefore possible to see an ex-Cooper vehicle working an ex-Green Bus service from the ex-Harper Brothers garage! The Heath Hayes garage can be seen in this late 1976 view; 2146 moved to the new garage at Cannock but was withdrawn soon after. *David Barber*

RIGHT Harpers opened 1966 with the introduction of two of these Leyland PD2A/27 Titans carrying 64-seat bodies by Metro-Cammell. Midland Red painted all the Leyland PD2 and PD3 Titans purchased new by Harpers into NBC poppy red. 2228 is seen on Brownhills Road in late 1976. *David Barber*

HEREFORD

Opened: 28 April 1925

To Midland Red West 6 September 1981, relaunched as First November 2001

Still in use.

Hereford was the furthest garage from the Birmingham heartland. The city remains full of architectural treasures with the Cathedral foremost. It remains associated with cider production and is the county town of an area famous for fruit and hopfields, pasture land and a breed of cattle.

Midland Red began operations in the city on 16 March 1920 but the original premises for the three Tilling-Stevens buses transferred to the city barely deserved the title 'garage'. The arrangements at the Black Lion Hotel on Bridge Street were very primitive with facilities for horses forming the paying-in office and stores! There was no lighting and the request to Head Office for illumination was met with a single hurricane lamp! With such a small fleet, a breakdown would leave two or three routes without a service but, fortunately, the allocation at Bridge Street grew to seven.

Land in Friar Street was purchased in 1920 and included a building containing three cottages, known as Chapel Cottages. The structure dated from the 17th century and was used in early days as a Quaker chapel. The three cottages had previously been

six dwellings and Midland Red continued the merging by adding two of the three together to form a house suitable for the foreman of the garage – Chief Engineer Shire liked to have senior staff close to the action! The first tenant was Mr E W Suddrick who had responsibility for the buses at the 'Black Lion'. He was one of the company's pioneers, having previously worked at Warwick, Bearwood and Banbury. Moving upwards in the organisation, he was Resident Engineer at Hereford until January 1945, later becoming Divisional Engineer based at Worcester until retiring in 1959. Mr Suddrick lived in the cottage until 1948 and was succeeded there by the Assistant Foreman. The cottages were demolished in the 1960s.

Mr Suddrick had to wait until April 1925 for the purpose-built, steel framed single bay garage on Friar Street to be completed. Extensions were opened in 1930 and 1940. Although the garage exterior was steel and asbestos sheeting, the look was softened by the attractive gardens bordering the long driveway. More land at the rear was purchased in 1947 to provide a vehicle park, enabling the allocation to approach 50 vehicles in the boom early post-war years. Various pieces of land for staff car parking further along Friar Street were bought and sold from 1956 onwards. The roof was raised where necessary in 1965, and the front entrance increased in height, to allow double-deck buses throughout the building.

The opening of the new garage brought the start of an expansion campaign at the expense of other operators' traffic. During this time Hereford Transport passed into the hands of the men developing the future Red & White group and soon after, on 29 November 1926, certain BMMO services based on Abergavenny, Monmouth and Ross-on-Wye were exchanged with Hereford Transport for services nearer Hereford. This was the first BMMO example of a mutually beneficial route exchange policy followed from time to time with neighbouring companies and small independent operators. While the general policy was expansion, Midland Red was also willing to dispose of unremunerative services if somebody else was prepared to take them on.

Hereford Transport was fully absorbed by Red & White in 1930.

Rationalisation agreements following the Road Traffic Act, 1930 included market services in the Hereford, Leominster and Kington areas being taken over from December 1934 by Yeomans Motors of Canon Pyon who were able to fit bus work in with their farming and cider making activities.

Hereford settled down to Midland Red providing the local city services and most country routes such as the X34/35 to Leominster, Ludlow and Shrewsbury, 440 to Hay-on-Wye, 468 to Ross-on-Wye, 477 to Ledbury and Great Malvern, and to Worcester via Ledbury (417) and Bromyard (420), among a raft of other highly rural operations. Red & White served destinations to the south-west and Yeomans to the north-west.

The 1928 service renumbering had allocated 422-78 to Hereford (479 was later used too). The six ex-Great Western Railway Maudslays were briefly operated from Hereford in 1930. The H prefix for local city services was introduced on 21 March 1932. These were more promising financially and provided work for double-deck buses introduced from 1950. The double-deck bus operations were relatively unchallenging so poorer power-to-weight ratio AD2 and D5B buses made up the majority of the allocation for many years. Later on, Fleetlines and Leopards were non-BMMO types to become familiar.

Many of the routes into the delightful rural hinterland would prove uneconomic as soon as passenger numbers started to decline. Narrow lanes meant a higher proportion of S6s lingered at Hereford. The combined problems of staff shortages, rising costs and poor patronage on many rural services meant Hereford was the first garage to introduce one-man-operated buses in 1956, in the form of S14s.

FAR LEFT An interior view of Hereford garage under construction in 1925, looking towards the front door. *The Transport Museum, Wythall collection*

BELOW 1954 C3 4208 was a regular at Hereford in its later years. The height of the garage has been increased by the time of this view - extra pieces have been added to the pillars and the cladding panels infilled to complete the job. *MRK Collection*

Deregulation began here!

'Wandaward' local branding was introduced on 11 March 1978 following a Market Analysis Project study. The once extensive network of Midland Red rural services was devastated by the MAP revisions which reduced the 36-strong allocation at Hereford by a third. More cuts followed in 1980 - it had become a desperate area to run buses, particularly if saddled with considerable central overheads. The NBC was addressing this by dividing the company but then the Conservative government decided to give its thoughts on bus service deregulation a first outing, Herefordshire County Council offering itself as a trial area, devoid of normal licensing procedures from 21 September 1981. Midland Red unsurprisingly was not happy with the concept and battened down its operations to a profitable core.

The successor Midland Red West thus began life in Hereford with reduced city services plus country routes only on the Leominster/ Ludlow/ Birmingham corridor, and via Bromyard to Worcester. With plenty of territory unserved, predictably competition was immediate on the only profitable services in the cathedral city. The situation was rather shambolic and the first challenger eventually had his licence revoked. On 9 April 1983, Midland Red West took over Yeomans activities on the city services. These included routes passed from one of the challengers only a few months previously, plus Yeomans' long-standing service to Credenhill. A new competitor immediately sprang up and Midland Red West hired and eventually purchased two Bedfords from Yeomans to assist in the latter's livery. Despite the clear evidence of network instability, deregulation was extended to the entire country in 1986 – except in London where there was (and still is) no risk of the downsides of deregulation being observed from the doors of the Houses of Parliament. As things settled, Midland Red West gained confidence and transport professionals everywhere have managed to work within the defective legislation imposed on them. Herefordshire's passengers have arguably done rather well, partly due to the supportive County Council. Midland Red West dropped the 'Wandaward' name from July 1984 but a minibus network using Mercedes-Benz vehicles with 'Hereford Hopper' branding was introduced from 23 April 1988.

ABOVE FAR LEFT The pride of the staff is demonstrated by this view of the landscaped approach drive. One family opposite the garage was so enamoured with the maintenance of the entrance that they named their dwelling 'Midland View'! In this picture the original part of the garage has not yet been increased in height. Dual-purpose 1963 LS18A Leopard/Willowbrook 5188 peeks out of the front entrance before it was raised for the double-deck buses that can be seen inside. As can be seen, the rear extension and entrance was built higher and provided the double-deck access. *Ken Jubb*

LEFT Recently washed 1936 SON 1917, with English Electric bodywork rebuilt by Aero & Engineering (Merseyside) at Hooton, stands at the end of the drive where the existence of the garage was flagged by the small sign. Chapel Cottages can be seen behind the bus. *The Transport Museum, Wythall*

TOP The Corporation constructed a bus station on Commercial Road in 1934 for operators' country services and this remains in use. It was built on the site of a former prison and the Prison Governor formerly occupied this building. Both Red & White and Midland Red had passenger enquiry offices in the building. It also held Midland Red's Traffic Offices for the town as the garage was over a mile away. The latter was thus purely an engineering establishment – a unique arrangement within the company. Red & White closed its bus station enquiry office and small garage in 1971 and then shared Midland Red's facilities but the latter also vacated the premises on 28 February 1979. The last S14 to enter service, no 4721 seen here, spent its entire life from 1959 to 1970 working at Hereford. *Ken Jubb*

ABOVE RIGHT 1936 SON 1911 (CHA 535) was used as a tree cutter from 1955 to 1963 and must have caused a surprise cruising through Hereford's bus station long after Midland Red's half-cab single-deckers had been retired from passenger service. *Ken Jubb*

RIGHT S9s 3372/4/85 were converted to tree cutters in 1963 and allocated to Bearwood, Leicester Southgate Street and Hereford respectively. 3385 remained on this work at Hereford until withdrawn in 1970. *Ken Jubb*

ABOVE S12 3761, with Metro-Cammell body intact and still in passenger service, provides a contrast to 3385 on the same day in 1966 and ran for a further year. *Ken Jubb*

BELOW It may not have lasted long in this form but this 1963 D9 with apples imaginatively added to its standard livery to promote a cider festival is probably one of Hereford's most fondly remembered buses. 5319, seen on a city service in May 1972, was not actually a Hereford bus but simply transferred for this job. *Ken Jubb*

LEFT The solitary Willowbrook-bodied S13, 3878, was a Hereford resident for most of its long life. *Ken Jubb*

BELOW LEFT For many years crews on the 112 mile long X91 Leicester – Hereford service did the full round trip. Tightening of drivers' hours regulations later meant that crews exchanged vehicles in each direction at Stratford-upon-Avon. The X91 ran only twice a day but was duplicated if necessary on busy days, on one occasion Alan Briggs saw twelve buses on one departure! Three S17s, 5722-4, were turned out in 1966 as dual-purpose prototypes with better quality seating, and were first classified S21A and then S22. No 5724 was allocated to Hereford and is a long way from home at Stratford-upon-Avon - the X91 was withdrawn when the trial area was introduced on 21 September 1981. The three buses were reclassified as S17s in 1971. *Ken Jubb*

BELOW Midland Red became desperately short of double-deckers and bought four of these ex-Trent 1971 Daimler Fleetline/Alexander buses immediately before the September 1981 split, three entering service with Midland Red West at Hereford and one with North at Ludlow. 'Wandaward' branded 2541 (a fleet number reviving fond memories of the D1 prototype) is seen near St Peter's on 28 April 1982, passing a Yeomans stop. All four Fleetlines moved to other garages, West selling 2541 to Midland Red North and its other two to South after 2-3 years. *Malcolm Keeley*

Hereford Cathedral provides the backdrop to Midland Red West 1975 Leyland National 397 on 21 May 1984, shortly before abandonment of 'Wandaward' branding. *Malcolm Keeley*

HINCKLEY

Opened: 1 January 1935
Closed: 12 May 1979

The garages in Leicester and Nuneaton were supplemented by this one in Hinckley, a town noted for the manufacturing of hosiery, footwear and other clothing. The red brick steel-framed building on Coventry Road had space for 50 vehicles. The H prefix for local services was introduced soon after opening, being first employed on 25 March 1935.

A large part of the garage was requisitioned during World War Two for aircraft component manufacture. There was some good news, however, as the Ministry of Aircraft Production extended it at the rear, BMMO acquiring this extension and increasing capacity to 60. Surplus space meant the company regularly parked stored and withdrawn vehicles here. Interesting temporary visitors in 1957 were the first twelve S15s, 4601-12, awaiting arrival of their dual-purpose quality seats from the manufacturer.

GHA-registered SONs were particularly familiar here. Double-deck buses were introduced in the 1950s, initially AD2s contributing to the busy 658 service between Leicester and Coventry, and its short workings. Other routes included to Leicester via Sapcote, the 754 (Nuneaton – Lutterworth) and the X62 (Coventry – Market Harborough). The garage was closed with the service economies brought with the introduction of the 'Hunter' network that covered both Nuneaton and Hinckley, and was later demolished.

ABOVE The introduction of a new route or conversion to double-deck buses required a Route Reconnaissance Report which recommended any actions to achieve safe operation. A tree-cutting vehicle was sometimes the solution but, in the case of the busy 658 service, it was lowering Hinckley Road, Nuneaton, beneath a bridge that removed the last obstacle. 1948 AD2 class AEC Regent II with Brush body 3133 received these opening ventilators in its front windows to address a problem of inadequate fresh air into the upper saloon. The solution adopted on most AD2s, and the D5s too, was vents in the front dome. 3133 was allocated to Hinckley and is seen, just before its July 1961 withdrawal, in the town's bus station. *Ken Jubb*

BELOW S13 3903 stands outside Hinckley garage in 1960. Services 725-727 were short workings of the 658 and adopted that number from 3 September 1966. The number 726 was reused as one of the rail replacement services introduced to Croft following closure of latter's railway station. *Ken Jubb*

RIGHT Hinckley garage had several duties for vehicles and crews operating both town and country services from Nuneaton. Standing at Stockingford Station is D7 4452, originally allocated to Leicester Sandacre but operated from Hinckley for its last four years before retirement in March 1971. The D7s were smooth and reliable but their Metro-Cammell bodies were rather cheap and nasty although their light weight meant that they were eager workhorses. This 1955 D7 is interesting because it had a non-standard front end including several features adopted on the D9. The windscreen was a single panel while the passenger window overlooking the bonnet had a curved lower edge, improving forward vision, and a hopper ventilator. *Steven Knight Photography/Midland Red Coaches Collection*

BELOW The maroon roof livery for dual-purpose vehicles did not last for long and looks unusual today. 1962 S15 5078 is seen in 1969, dressed for a local service. *Ken Jubb*

KIDDERMINSTER

Opened: 30 May 1930

To Midland Red West 6 September 1981, relaunched as First November 2001

Closed: 2 June 2001

Formerly known as a great centre of carpet manufacturing, among other industries, Kidderminster was a very early example of BET operations in the Midlands, electric tramways running to Stourport as early as 1898. Motorbuses operated by the BET-owned tramway company in Kidderminster began in 1913. On 14 August 1914 the Worcestershire Motor Transport Company, Ltd was formed to combine and develop the bus interests of the BET tramways at Worcester and Kidderminster. Unfortunately, only two months later the War Office requisitioned the majority of its vehicles upon the outbreak of World War One. The military did not like the Tilling-Stevens buses operated by Midland Red which was accordingly handed in November 1914 a ready-made service network with accommodation initially in the tram depot off New Road of the Kidderminster District Lighting & Traction Co Ltd, and then in an adjoining building. The ex-WMT bodies from the Leyland chassis taken by the military were fitted to new Midland Red Tilling-Stevens TS3 chassis in 1915 and, appropriately, some of these were allocated to Kidderminster. Midland Red buses replaced the Kidderminster to Stourport tramway in November 1928.

A purpose-built replacement garage in New Road was opened on 30 May 1930, capable of accommodating forty buses of the time. This was a steel-frame structure with red brick frontage and two-storey office buildings. The November 1938 takeover of P Owen & Sons, Abberley, included the small garage in George Street which was rented out until being requisitioned during World War Two by the Ministry of Aircraft Production. The George Street premises were last used by BMMO in August 1956 and sold in 1957.

The post-World War Two growth meant 62 vehicles were allocated to Kidderminster by 1955, well in excess of the New Road garage's capacity. George Street provided overnight space for seven and the remainder rested on the municipal car park in New Road. The solution came with purchases of land adjacent to the New Road garage in 1945 and 1955, the latter giving direct access onto Corporation Street where many bus services terminated. The garage could then be modernised and extended, which increased capacity to 63 vehicles, the work being completed in 1962. The concrete clad, steel-framed brick extension included a factory building on the floor above, taking maximum advantage of the land area. This was rented by Brintons, the carpet manufacturers, and was accessed from their adjacent premises.

The 1928 service renumbering allocated 288-317 to Kidderminster and K prefixes for local services were introduced on 30 November 1931. The garage contributed

buses to important routes passing through the town such as those from Birmingham on their way to Stourport, Bewdley and Ludlow, and on the Wolverhampton – Stourbridge – Worcester corridor. Rural services included those to Bridgnorth and Tenbury Wells.

A batch of consecutive D5Bs, 3814-9, received in 1951 was followed two years later by several LD8s that fitted nicely with the subsequent LS18s. The Market Analysis Project brought 'Wendaway' local branding, introduced on 5 November 1977 but discontinued from July 1984.

Shropshire was allocated to Midland Red North upon the 1981 split but retrenchment exercises in May 1983 and April 1987 gave opportunities to West with buses being taken over on both occasions. Since 1983 Kidderminster buses have been outstationed in various towns. A fleet of Mercedes-Benz minibuses was introduced to Kidderminster and Stourport from 8 March 1986, branded 'Wyre Forest Shuttle'.

New Road garage was replaced by new accommodation in the town, featuring largely open parking. Both New Road and George Street premises have been demolished.

ABOVE FAR LEFT The ex-Owen premises in George Street on 13 October 1938. The awkward access meant Midland Red never used it for regular operations. *BMMO*

FAR LEFT S14 4584 awaits its next duty on 25 May 1963 in Corporation Street when working local services. The direct access from the recently extended garage can be seen in the background. *Andrew Willis*

TOP Former Worcester - Birmingham motorway coach 4834 revisits the scene of its glory days at Worcester's Newport Street bus station but instead will be working a stage service back to Kidderminster in early 1969. Its bland style of fleetname was used on the DD12 Daimler Fleetlines when new as well as some downgraded C5 coaches. *Ken Jubb*

ABOVE St John's Road, Stourbridge, is being transformed into part of the town's ring road as S23 5957 reaches journey's end from Kidderminster on 30 April 1974. Stourbridge garage passed to West Midlands PTE the previous December and has on loan the ex-Birmingham City Transport 1952 Daimler CVG6 seen in the background on service S56 from Norton estate. *Malcolm Keeley*

ABOVE 1977 dual-purpose Plaxton-bodied Leyland Leopard 671 has just crossed Bewdley's graceful three-arch bridge over the River Severn, built by Thomas Telford, one of the greatest engineers and road builders of all time, and is standing in the appropriately named Load Street. The Midland Express branding was launched on 28 March 1983 to reduce confusion on the limited stop network operated by the four Midland Red successor bus companies. By the date of this photograph, 28 March 1990, deregulation had frowned on co-operation as uncompetitive, the original standard branded livery had gone and only West maintained the Midland Express name. Midland Red West differentiated its express buses by applying this yellow instead of off-white to its standard livery. *Malcolm Keeley*

RIGHT 1987 Mercedes-Benz 609D 1408 travels down Comberton Hill while one of the original Shuttle minibuses, 1986 L608D 1367, labours in the opposite direction on 29 September 1989. Both have 20-seat bodies converted by Reeve Burgess. *Malcolm Keeley*

LEFT The 1970 Leyland Leopard coaches (Midland Red C11 class 6226-55) had Plaxton bodies built to a pre-Elite style and looked rather old-fashioned. Midland Red Express had 6249/51/4/5 rebodied by ECW, the vehicles being re-registered ROG 549-552Y and re-entering service in early 1983. In the summer and autumn of 1989 they were equipped for stage carriage services, reliveried as Midland Express vehicles and transferred to Kidderminster. They displaced Leopards with older bodies that were downgraded to bus service livery for country services although retaining coach seats. No 552 approaches Far Forest from Ludlow on service 192 on 29 March 1995, its chassis now 25 years old; one cannot help recalling 1950s bank holidays when this would have been a double-decker packed to the gunwales. *Malcolm Keeley*

KINETON

Stratford Blue, a Midland Red subsidiary from 1935, may have been a small fleet with around 40 vehicles but it had a second garage in addition to its Stratford premises. Continuing a rainbow theme from Midland Red to Stratford Blue, we come to Kineton Green. Stratford Blue took over Kineton Green Bus Services with effect from 1 January 1937, including its garage in Brookhampton Lane which had been rebuilt after a serious fire in 1934. No Kineton Green buses were kept, being replaced by secondhand Tilling-Stevens vehicles. Stratford Blue thus had a group of services based around Kineton, including from 1937 more routes to Banbury, handed over by Midland Red who had acquired them in 1935 from F E Bloxham of Tysoe.

Six single-deckers could be accommodated in the ex-Kineton Green garage. This became inadequate in the post-war years, particularly after the arrival of the Leyland double-deckers. A new garage opened on 1 February 1954, alongside and replacing the existing one, capable of holding twelve buses of the time. Running repairs were conducted at Kineton but major maintenance was done at Stratford. Kineton garage still had 12 vehicles at transfer to Midland Red on 1 January 1971. It survived the introduction of the 'Avonbus' network and branding introduced on 28 May 1977 but succumbed under the 'Leamington & Warwick' scheme.

ABOVE Outside the garage opened in 1954 is no 48, a 1948 Leyland Tiger PS1 with Northern Coach Builders body. *Ken Jubb*

BELOW No 54, a Leyland Tiger PS2 with 34-seat Willowbrook body, stands inside Kineton garage. There were six of these Leylands received in 1950, two including no 54 with bus seating, the remaining four to dual-purpose standard. They were rendered obsolete by underfloor-engine designs and the pressing need on Stratford Blue's rural routes to move towards driver only operation. The Leyland chassis were sound so five were rebodied as double-deckers (see pages 133-4). No 54 remained unrebuilt and became the last half-cab single-decker with Stratford Blue, being withdrawn in 1963. *Ken Jubb*

ABOVE LEFT For a small fleet, it was strange that Stratford Blue was fond of reusing fleet numbers. This is the replacement no 47, one of four 1960 Leyland Tiger Cubs with Park Royal 45-seat bodies particularly associated with Kineton garage, seen at Banbury Bus Sation in 1970. *Ken Jubb*

LEFT No 59 was an exquisite 1966 Leyland L2T with Marshall 41-seat coachwork, its greater area of cream identifying its dual-purpose specification. Stratford Blue used white instead of cream from around 1969. This bus

lasted well as 2059 in the Midland Red fleet and was transferred to Ludlow in November 1977. Midland Red West employed it as a trainer for very many years until it passed into preservation. *Ken Jubb*

ABOVE New Ford R192/ Plaxton 6385 has been allocated to Kineton in 1971 and is on its way to the nearby military establishment. 34 is an ex-Stratford Blue service number; Kineton's bus services were revised and renumbered into the 5xx series from 9 October 1971, Stratford following on 1 January 1972. *Ken Jubb*

KINGSWINFORD

Opened: 2 April 1917
Closed: 4 November 1932

The purchase of the Wolverhampton – Kingswinford - Brettell Lane service of C. L. Wells Ltd of Kingswinford included a small garage on The Portway. This was an old red brick building with wooden roof and could accommodate around 20 single-deckers.

The Kingswinford garage in September 1929 with its external fuelling point on the driveway. *BMMO*

LEAMINGTON & WARWICK EMSCOTE

Opened: 5 December 1914
Closed: 31 August 1957

The Leamington & Warwick Tramways Co Ltd built the Emscote depot to accommodate its tramcars which were horse-drawn when operations began in 1881. The tramways were electrified around 1905, Emscote gaining an electricity generating station which would be retained by the subsequent electricity authorities.

The company, by now owned by the BET, also developed bus services to complement the tramway system. The buses and services were sold in 1912 to another BET subsidiary, the British Automobile Traction Co, while the tramways passed to a subsidiary of the Balfour Beatty group. The 'British' buses were transferred soon after the outbreak of World War One to other parts of the country in order to maintain routes considered more vital to the war effort. The services were thus handed over on 5 December 1914 to BMMO who occupied part of the Emscote premises until opening its own garage on Old Warwick Road, Leamington, in April 1922 – approximately ten buses being transferred from Emscote.

The tramway company was renamed the Leamington & Warwick Transport Co and replaced its trams in 1933 with buses in a green livery. Midland Red bought the company from the Balfour Beatty group in 1935, running it as a subsidiary until its own buses took over on 1 October 1937. None of the absorbed subsidiary's buses ran for Midland Red. However, the assortment of steel framed brick and corrugated iron buildings that comprised the premises at Emscote returned to the fold on lease by becoming an overflow garage for Leamington's Old Warwick Road site.

Emscote garage was closed as services were cut upon the outbreak of World War Two but reopened as Leamington came under enormous pressure following the Coventry blitz. As an overflow dormitory garage, its allocation was basically elderly single-deckers but its importance increased in the post-war travel boom, especially from 1950 when double-deckers were introduced to the area and were impossible to accommodate at Old Warwick Road. Alongside BMMO types, AD2s and LD8s made up a considerable proportion of the 35 buses transferred when Emscote was replaced by a new garage in Myton Road, Leamington.

A great view of FEDD 2220 outside Emscote garage. *MRK collection*

LEAMINGTON OLD WARWICK ROAD

Opened: April 1922
Closed: 30 May 1980

The mineral springs brought a succession of royal personages to Leamington to take the waters, including Queen Victoria who granted the town the right to call itself Royal Leamington Spa. The result of this patronage is a Regency town centre with tree-lined wide streets and spacious gardens. Twentieth century growth was rather different with a lot of industry and Leamington has now far outstripped the county town of Warwick next door in size.

Midland Red constructed one of its earliest purpose-designed garages on Old Warwick Road, in this case for 25 vehicles, unfortunately too early to consider the concept of closed top double-deck buses. The steel-framed red brick garage in 1925 needed the first of its two extensions, on both occasions achieved by the addition of extra bays resulting in a new capacity of 50, soon reduced to 45 as buses got larger.

Midland Red allocated the numbers 513-575 to Leamington and Stratford services but, in time, the reservation was nibbled at both ends with Banbury taking up to 516 and Rugby 570 onwards.

Midland Red bought the Leamington & Warwick Transport Co from Balfour Beatty in 1935, running the green-liveried buses as a subsidiary until 1 October 1937. On that date Midland Red introduced L prefix local services in Leamington and Warwick, operated by a considerable number of new DHA-registered SONs allocated to Leamington garage. None of the absorbed subsidiary's buses ran for Midland Red but the Leamington & Warwick company

A view of Old Warwick Road garage around 1952. Those prominent letters stood out clearly against the skyline to users of the Great Western Railway station across the road. Just visible is a little hut alongside the garage entrance. This was used by the trade union to collect subscriptions – Midland Red would not allow this to be carried on inside company premises. *BMMO*

continued to exist as the two Corporations had powers to purchase the undertaking at seven year intervals. Midland Red continued to pay its non-operating subsidiary company the net profits on the routes taken over, on the proportionate route mileage basis pioneered at Worcester. Old Warwick Road was already responsible for services to places further afield, particularly Coventry and Stratford but also including Rugby, Birmingham, Southam and Stockton.

Leamington came under enormous pressure following the Coventry blitz. To assist the increased demand, all 31 members of the LRR class eventually gathered at Leamington - these high-geared former coaches being ideal for the open roads between Coventry and nearby towns.

The opening of Myton Road garage in 1957 relieved pressure on Old Warwick Road but the disadvantages of fragmented operational control meant thoughts of replacing both garages with one were being considered as early as 1969. In the event service cuts brought the end of Old Warwick Road garage. The building survived into the 21st century but has since been demolished.

ABOVE Staff at the new garage with two Tilling-Stevens buses in 1922.
The Transport Museum, Wythall collection

BELOW A somewhat lonely S6 3098 poses in Old Warwick Road garage on 25 May 1963. All engineering was concentrated at Myton Road after its opening so the pits here were covered over with railway sleepers bought from British Railways at Swindon. *Andrew Willis*

LEAMINGTON MYTON ROAD

Opened: 1 September 1957
To Midland Red South 6 September 1981
Closed: 27 January 1991

The land in Myton Road was purchased in July 1936 but, with World War Two, post-war building restrictions and more pressing problems elsewhere, the new garage was not opened until 1957. When it finally arrived, it was a classic example of Midland Red post-war architectural styling with capacity for 65 vehicles. The roof was supported by tubular steel framework and included translucent reinforced glass fibre roof panels. The yard had facilities for steam cleaning the underside of buses. Myton Road garage replaced Emscote and relieved Old Warwick Road – all maintenance now being undertaken at the new garage.

TOP The new garage on Myton Road in 1957. *BMMO*

RIGHT 1940 SON 2429 (GHA 348) was used as a tree cutter and towing bus at Leamington from 1958 to 1963. Sharing the yard in 1960 is one of only two S13s with Carlyle bodies, prototypes new in 1951. This is 3877 which, unlike most S13s, had 44 bus seats instead of 40 more luxurious dual-purpose ones. It worked most of its life at Leamington. *Ken Jubb*

Before the arrival of bigger buses, D5B and D7 buses were very familiar here but approximately equalled in numbers by members of the Leyland LD8 class, great 'open road' buses largely replaced by new D9s and Daimler Fleetlines 5992-6011 in 1966. Single-deckers particularly included S8, S10 and S13 types and earlier S14s. As an established Leyland garage, Leamington also received a generous number of LS18s in 1963.

The opening of a Ford plant just down the road was a mixed blessing, bringing new passengers but in due course adding to staff recruitment and retention problems caused by the many buoyant car factories then in nearby Coventry. Consequently one of the interesting features of Leamington operations for many years was the hiring of buses with drivers, particularly from G & G Coaches, which purchased two ex-Leamington LD8s and used them on this work.

The wheel went almost full circle when the local identity name 'Leamington & Warwick' was introduced after MAP. Myton Road garage was sold for redevelopment, being replaced in June 1990 by new premises in Station Approach that also would accommodate the vehicles of G & G Coaches which had been a sister company since MRS's owner Western Travel had acquired it the previous year. A problem at Station Approach meant Myton Road was re-opened for large buses, delaying its final closure. It has since been demolished.

ABOVE GHA 348's replacement in 1963 was this handsome conversion of D5 3508. *Ken Jubb*

BELOW The early post-war fleet had been withdrawn from passenger service by mid-1967 but 1950 S10 3635 survived as a towing vehicle. It arrived at Leamington in May 1969 to replace D5 3508, transferred to Birmingham. Note it had received the small fleet numbers then being applied to newer buses in the fleet. None of the chassisless generation of single-deckers (S14-S23) were used as towing vehicles, the next generation would be D7s followed by Leyland Leopards. *Ken Jubb*

ABOVE Good reason to travel to Leamington in the early 1960s was to catch sight of the solitary 1939 ONC dual-control trainer, 2273 (FHA 405), here tracked down in Warwick. *Tim Meredith*

LEFT 1949 C1 coach 3311 was converted to a dual-control tuition vehicle in 1962 and arrived at Leamington in 1965, being seen here early in 1967. 3311 received the C5 livery in its new role, a style not applied to any in passenger service. It was not withdrawn until 1975 and became a hospitality vehicle before being preserved by Colin Hawketts. *Ken Jubb*

BELOW LEFT The council opened the bus station in Avenue Road on Saturday 3 December 1960 – Midland Red basically used it for country routes rather than town services. The 1953 LD8 class Leylands were ideal for Leamington's operations and many ran from here. No 4002 was a late arrival at Myton Road, however, being allocated elsewhere until May 1964. It is seen in the bus station in 1966. *Ken Jubb*

ABOVE Red and black suited the 49 Duple-bodied Leyland Leopard coaches delivered in 1965 as the LC7 class. Looks like a case of April showers for 5799 in 1967. *Ken Jubb*

RIGHT One does not associate the ex-Midland Red companies with open-top sightseeing buses but MRS did dabble. Daimler Fleetline/ Alexander 990, formerly bus 6095, is seen at Hales Street, Coventry on 14 June 1986. *Malcolm Keeley*

BELOW Leamington's tow truck Q341 GVC, once Midland Red Leopard/ Plaxton tour coach 5830, brings home an ex-Greater Manchester 1974 Daimler Fleetline with Northern Counties body needing first aid on 6 August 1988. Four of these Fleetlines had been purchased earlier that year and replaced at Leamington an earlier generation of secondhand Northern Counties-bodied Fleetlines, this time ex-West Riding. *Malcolm Keeley*

LEICESTER EARLY PREMISES

The most important challenge for Midland Red after the First World War was arguably Leicestershire where the company began a determined campaign and had to fight, occasionally literally, to gain pre-eminence. Although Leicester was to become one of the Company's largest and most prosperous areas of operation with over 10% of the fleet based there, it was not until 1922 that a garage was opened.

The first BMMO service to reach Leicester was the 68 Nuneaton – Earl Shilton service, extended to Leicester on 11 May 1921, worked out of Nuneaton garage. This was followed on 4 June by a service from Coventry, worked by that city's garage and from 15 July from Burton, worked by Tamworth garage. Premises were rented on Frog Island, near Slater Street in Leicester, opening on 26 August 1922, primarily for a new network of services commenced in September and October. This was capable of holding thirty vehicles but was soon overcrowded so further leased premises, accommodating a further ten, were obtained in Welford Road in May 1925, although all maintenance continued to be handled at Frog Island. The Leicester allocation included some of the company's Tilling-Stevens double-deck forward control conversions; these tended towards Welford Road after that was obtained. By the time Southgate Street garage opened, the Leicester-Nuneaton service was running every 10 minutes and carried 300,000 passengers every week. Frog Island and Welford Road were replaced by Southgate Street after 20 July 1927.

SMOKING NOT ALLOWED

The introduction of the company's buses to Leicester highlighted that the competition was often armed with small, fast, lightweight buses that ran proverbial rings around the Midland 'Red' Tilling-Stevens petrol-electrics. Mr Shire, Midland Red's Chief Engineer, was conscious of this shortcoming and, after bus manufacturers failed to meet his requirement for vehicles that combined the capacity of the Tillings with the nimbleness of the small 'opposition' buses, he took the historic decision that the Company would design and build its own buses. This is the Frog Island garage around 1926 and SOS buses are replacing the earlier Tilling-Stevens models. These premises still stand at the time of writing.
The Transport Museum, Wythall, archive

LEICESTER SOUTHGATE STREET

Opened: 21 July 1927

To Midland Red East 6 September 1981; relaunched as Midland Fox January 1984, relaunched as Arriva 1997

Closed: 12 July 2009

Southgate Street should have been available by Christmas 1926 but the General Strike of that year caused numerous delays, not least to the steelwork. The official opening ceremony for Southgate Street was held on 27 June 1927 and was an impressive affair, including a show chassis alongside examples of the latest completed vehicles.

The new garage was on a corner site with Peacock Lane. The corner remained open, sitting in the elbow of the garage which was L-shaped. The open section formed a bus and coach station much employed by trippers and holidaymakers to Skegness and Great Yarmouth, and the terminus of certain longer bus services. A brick Booking and Enquiry Office was provided here, originally separate but later connected to the garage.

The garage itself was capable of accommodating around 90 vehicles and was the company's first large premises with a single span roof, stretching 120 feet without support pillars. The side facing Peacock Lane was rather grand, with a decorative exit to the garage. The three storey red brick office building next

door at 12 Peacock Lane became available and was purchased in the mid-1930s. The Southgate Street entrance was a great contrast, being painted steel or asbestos panelling. There was a third access from Friar Lane, suitable for pedestrians and cycles only. Leicester existed in Roman times and excavations for the inspection pits revealed a tessellated pavement that was removed to Leicester Museum.

The service renumbering in February 1928 saw the numbers 601-724 allocated to the Leicester, Coalville and Ashby areas, although the numbers crept backwards to 598. Network growth had become constrained from November 1927 as the City Police established order by reducing the number of termini and grouping destinations among them, and introducing stringent conditions on timekeeping. In 1928 there were 399 opposition vehicles, spread among 95 operators, plying for hire on routes run by Midland Red. Late buses had to miss their slots and were sent away empty. This proved a big penalty for hanging back onto another proprietor's time and

the weaker withdrew, often selling goodwill to Midland Red. Taking over existing activities now became the main means of growth, especially after service regulation was brought by the Road Traffic Act, 1930. Co-ordination agreements over certain corridors were struck with many local independent operators in 1931-2; some of the independents remained for many years - a few surviving into bus service deregulation from 1986.

The 1930 Act was also the opportunity for Leicester Corporation to apply for protection to its bus and tram routes to prevent any other operator from picking up inbound passengers and requiring a minimum fare to be applied to those travelling outwards. Midland Red duly contested and managed to confine Leicester City Transport to certain areas, keeping some areas largely to itself, obtained some useful services and agreed the protection points with the Corporation on the majority. The Corporation was then obliged to make deals when the city boundaries were extended, Midland Red retaining or securing strength in certain areas of the city, notably Braunstone, New Parks and Thurnby Lodge housing estates. The L local service prefix was introduced on 8 February 1932 but became disused forty years later as co-ordination with the corporation increased.

The Leicester & District Bus Company was acquired on 1 November 1936. With insufficient Midland Red vehicles available and bearing in mind the good maintenance of Leicester Green (as the fleet was known), contrary to normal practice BMMO actually took over and operated some of the Albion vehicles, still in their green livery, with "MIDLAND" fleetnames. Among other things, Midland Red obtained complete control of the corridors to Hinckley and Syston, the latter following a simultaneous deal and route exchange with C H Allen of Mountsorrel.

After the opening of Sandacre Street, Southgate Street retained a lot of the longer distance work, with stage services

FAR LEFT 1530 (HA 9481) was one of Midland Red's prototype diesel buses, classified DON when new in 1934. It became Southgate Street's tree cutter for many years from 1951 until 1963, most of the time the only survivor with the company carrying a registration with two letters preceding four numbers. This made no 1530 seem unbelievably old, the writer remembers catching first sight of it as a youth and thinking it awesome. This atmospheric shot in the garage shows it in 1960 - the line of parked coaches may indicate this is winter. *Ken Jubb*

ABOVE A view of Southgate Street garage from the Peacock Lane end. *BMMO*

BELOW Midland Red buses rubbed shoulders with those of Barton, Lincolnshire Road Car and United Counties at Southgate Street plus, of course, the long distance departures. Non-BMMO vehicles in this view from around 1960 include a Bristol L and a Barton AEC Reliance leaving the yard with, behind them, a Lincolnshire Bristol LS and a Midland Red Austin A35 van, possibly belonging to the painter attending to the windows – the garage cladding is partly repainted. In 1967 daily stage service departures from the yard comprised 17 Southgate Street and ten Birmingham Digbeth journeys (X68) plus one each from Sandacre Street, Wigston, Hereford (X91) and Shrewsbury garages (X97). Lincolnshire accounted for four more and United Counties one. *BMMO*

to Hereford, Birmingham, Coventry, Melton Mowbray and Grantham, as well as Nuneaton, Coalville, Lutterworth and Market Harborough, shorter distance and L-prefix local services. Southgate Street included Drivers' and Conductors' Training Schools for the Leicester area.

Leicester has always required double-deck buses even though at times the management seemed to think the company could manage without them! Some of the Tilling-Stevens front-entrance double-deckers were here and the first production batch of SOS double-deckers, the 1932-3 REDDs, were particularly significant for many years. In addition to SOS/BMMO types were AD2s and, later, Leopards and Fleetlines.

Midland Red East reversed the old company's chronic trend towards single-deckers largely with secondhand buses, particularly ex-London Fleetlines. It imaginatively renamed itself Midland Fox on 16 January 1984 and broke away from the rigorously imposed NBC livery directives, also introducing marketing initiatives amid a recast and renumbered Leicester network. All the Leicester City Transport restrictions were lifted from 1 July 1984 after Midland Fox management had launched and won a court case. The double-deckers, combined with a large number of minibuses, meant Fox was able to give Leicester's municipally owned bus undertaking a hard time upon deregulation in 1986.

Southgate Street's employment as a terminus was much reduced in 1968 when country bus services were transferred to St Margaret's and ceased in Spring 1980 when the coach services followed. In later years the garage was familiarly known as 'Southgates'. The last conductors on Midland Red were at Southgates and finished on 31 May 1980, the last half-cab buses in the form of D9s having been withdrawn at the end of the previous year. On closure, services were passed to Arriva garages at Coalville, Thurmaston and Wigston and the garage was demolished soon after.

TOP This Leicester Green Albion was photographed at Southgate Street carrying the MIDLAND fleetname. JF 4873 was a PV70 model with Duple 35-seat coachwork new in 1933, one of a pair that were the newest vehicles in the Leicester Green fleet. It is correctly dressed for the 645 route between Earl Shilton and Leicester, complete with number stencil and slipboard via Thurlaston and Enderby. *BMMO*

ABOVE 8 feet wide buses were permitted from the late 1940s but their routes needed special authorisation for some years. Because they could be required to go almost anywhere, the C1 and C2 coaches were thus built to the earlier width of 7 feet 6 inches. However, Midland Red started construction of 8 feet wide service buses as soon as possible, beginning with the S8. Keen BMMO aficionados will have spotted that the front styling was subtly changed between the S6 and the wider S8. This view of Southgate Street's S6 3042, seen at the far end of the X91 at Hereford, will therefore surprise because it has the S8 styling albeit, presumably, with slightly narrower glasses. The bus is still young, was it built like this as the styling prototype for the wider buses? *MRK Collection*

ABOVE Looking in the opposite direction provides a good view of the Booking and Enquiry Office in 1969. The attractive Office would have looked more at home in a rural town but the painters have been busy again, making the rest of the architecturally grim coach station look as appealing as possible. *Ken Jubb*

RIGHT 1965 LC7 class Leyland Leopard PSU3/4R with Duple 'Commander' body 5795 was used as the Leicester City Football Club team coach for several winters until replaced on this work in 1969 by LC10 Leopard/ Plaxton 6153. The LC7's seating capacity was reduced from 49 to 41 including some seats facing backwards around tables. *Ken Jubb*

BELOW RIGHT Seven double-deck buses were purchased from Potteries Motor Traction in 1979 but any hopes that these would stem the gradual loss of high capacity vehicles was dashed when only one entered service and that very briefly. Numbered 2910 (910 UVT) in the Midland Red fleet, the 1962 Leyland Atlantean with Weymann 73-seat body was seen here on 14 April 1979. *Malcolm Keeley*

ABOVE The availability of a bus grant in the 1970s to speed modernisation of the industry and extend driver-only operation meant many companies hesitated before overhauling or repairing half-cab buses when the second Certificate of Fitness expired at the age of twelve years. D9 4975 is seen near the start of an operational life that began in April 1962 but ended in May 1973, mostly running from Southgate Street. *T C Bassindale/ The Transport Museum, Wythall*

RIGHT Several Midland Red Express Leyland Leopard/ Plaxton coaches were transferred to Midland Red East from 1 January 1982 when it was decided the Leicester area should cater for its own National Express and National Holidays work. These coaches were well looked after, including wheel trims as demonstrated by 611, new in 1976, at Southgate Street on 17 March 1984. *Malcolm Keeley*

LEICESTER HASTINGS ROAD

Opened: July 1932
Closed: 31 January 1937

Midland Red had premises in Hastings Road, Humberstone, on a five-year lease commencing 25 July 1932 to assist the shortage of vehicle accommodation in Leicester. The garage was no longer required after the opening of Sandacre Street.

This is believed to be the Hastings Road premises. The tenancy agreement refers to an electric crane that will remain the property of the landlord, F W C Bowles of Bowles & Son, Builders, Contractors & Decorators, who may maintain or remove it at any time during the period of the tenancy. Such a crane is visible here, along with a Q type on the left, possibly HA 3627 or 3637, and MM HA 5062. *MRK collection*

LEICESTER SANDACRE STREET

Opened: 1 February 1937
To Midland Red East 6 September 1981; relaunched as Midland Fox January 1984
Closed: 24 September 1995

This further large 70-vehicle garage, familiarly called 'Sandacre', was ideally located in the city centre with St Margaret's Bus Station being opened on the other side of Gravel Street a few years later. The garage had entrances and exits on Gravel Street, Sandacre Street and Mansfield Street to the rear. It was built in the classic Midland Red fashion of its period with steel frame, red brick and stone facings. It had a brick-built clock tower over the Enquiry Office which had a brick portico softened with hanging baskets. The office block extended along the Gravel Street frontage.

Services allocated to the new garage tended to be those to the north and east of the city including routes to Loughborough,

Melton Mowbray, Uppingham, and to Oakham in the tiny county of Rutland, plus a selection of locals. The opening allocation included the six ex-Leicester & District Albions transferred from Southgate Street. Most of the 1932-3 REDDs not at Southgate Street would be found here. Sandacre was one of two garages with wartime Guys, although the first few were briefly operated by Southgate Street. Of the post-war double-deckers, all the numerous types were here including many AD2s, with LD8s arriving in their final months.

The founder of the bus company Allen of Mountsorrel, which also owned Kemp & Shaw, died in 1954. The following year Midland Red took over Allen's services from Leicester to Loughborough and Derby, and purchased the whole of the share capital of Allen subsidiary Kemp & Shaw. The latter was run as a BMMO subsidiary and the Kemp & Shaw buses were transferred to Sandacre from their garage in Thurcaston Road. Kemp & Shaw was absorbed in 1959 when, unusually for Midland Red, its surviving Guy and Leyland buses were taken into the fleet, repainted red and numbered 4838-45. Another operator, H. Boyer & Son, was acquired the same year and again their buses entered the fleet, two Sentinels and a Leyland numbered 4846-8.

A tempting duo at Sandacre in the early post-war years. 1774 (BHA 329) is a 1936 Metro-Cammell bodied FEDD while 3123 (JHA 24) is a 1948 Brush-bodied AEC Regent II, one of the AD2 class. The latter's previous journey was on the X68 from Birmingham, taking the pretty route between Coventry and Leicester via Wolvey and Sharnford. *The Transport Museum, Wythall*

Subsidy cuts in Leicestershire led to major reductions on 31 May 1980, including the closure of Sandacre Street. At the time of the transfer to Midland Red East, the company was using the garage as a public car park. Midland Fox placed a huge number of Ford Transit 'Fox Cub' minibuses into service prior to deregulation, introducing them to Leicester in September 1985. The expanding minibus fleet in the city was concentrated at Sandacre, reopened for them in 1986. The garage was replaced by a site in Thurmaston, subsequently consolidated and redeveloped as the headquarters of Arriva's local operations.

TOP With more buses than the garages could accommodate, Midland Red took advantage of a cleared site in Abbey Street and Archdeacon Lane for daytime parking. Sandacre's allocation of wartime Guys had bodies by a variety of builders who mostly had to use frames of unseasoned wood, causing the bodies to need heavy rebuilding later. The Northern Counties bodies, represented here by no 2586 and contrasting with the bodies of the Guys around it, were metal-framed and robust. They only received the modernisations required to soften the austerity features although the jury is still out on whether the built-up front wings were really an improvement. *Gordon Davies*

ABOVE Kemp & Shaw provided six Guy Arabs, four with Northern Counties double-deck bodies and two single-deckers with rare Barnards bodies (see Shrewsbury garage for one of the latter). The oldest was DJF 392, an Arab with the Mark II radiator position but actually a Mark III, delivered in March 1946, and the only one with half drop ventilators. It is seen here as Midland Red 4838 in 1960. *Ken Jubb*

LEFT One of Sandacre Street's celebrity buses was the 'American' S9 3441. It was passed for service in March 1950 with this redesigned front end, becoming the company's first single-decker with electronically operated platform doors. Cab access was via the saloon instead of a separate door on the offside and, on all the early power-door single-deckers, the driver was separated from the passengers by only a waist-high partition, giving a light and airy ambience with excellent forward vision. After trials at Bearwood and Cradley Heath garages, 3441 was transferred to Sandacre Street where, in October of that year, it would introduce the new X97 service between Leicester and Shrewsbury. The generous brightwork was a feature of Midland Red prototypes around this time. It was withdrawn in 1963, still working from Sandacre. Conductors would have to watch their blinds; Leicester buses served Thurcaston, Thurlaston and Thurmaston! *Ken Jubb*

ABOVE RIGHT Sandacre Street was handily adjacent to St Margaret's Bus Station, originally known as Gravel Street. The first phase of the bus station opened at the height of World War Two in July 1942. AD2 3117 awaits its next work and has Ratby on the rear destination blind. The -by suffix is from the Danish for small settlement, the county had clearly been invaded by the Danes, Leicester blinds also including Arnesby, Asfordby, Barkby, Blaby, Cosby, Enderby, Gaddesby, Goadby, Oadby, Rearsby, Shearsby, Sileby, Somerby, Thurnby, Tugby and perhaps Rugby, Ashby Folville and Kirby Muxloe can be included too! *Ken Jubb*

RIGHT EBC 882 was the next Guy Arab III/ Northern Counties delivery to Kemp & Shaw in December 1946 and was followed by EJF 668-9 in November 1947. They became 4839-41. This useful shot not only shows the rear of 4839 (and 4841 in front of it) but also the decorative corner containing the passenger enquiry office of Sandacre Street garage. The four Kemp & Shaw Guy double-deckers were out of service by early 1961. *Ken Jubb*

ABOVE The secondhand buses from Kemp & Shaw and Boyer were quickly repainted in the early months of 1959. Here 1950 Leyland-bodied PD2 4844 (GRY 763), the only true 'lowbridge' double-deck bus in the Midland Red fleet, still carries Kemp & Shaw colours but, around it in Sandacre garage, is an Kemp & Shaw Guy and an ex-Boyer Sentinel already in Midland Red livery. 4844 ran with Midland Red until June 1967 and was then sold to a Birmingham driving school. *Ken Jubb*

BELOW Sandacre garage stretches behind ex-Boyer 1951 Sentinel STC4 44-seater 4846 (HAW 578) at St Margaret's. This Sentinel was retained until 1963. *The Transport Museum, Wythall*

ABOVE The size of Midland Red's territory was remarkable when you consider how far Melton Mowbray, seen here, is from the company's heartland in Birmingham, let alone Herefordshire. 1964 S17 5587 is rubbing shoulders in 1969 with one of Barton's large fleet of forward entrance Leyland PD1 Titans with Duple bodies, by then twenty years old. *Ken Jubb*

LEFT St Margaret's saw buses of Barton and Trent, and smaller independent operators. The road to Loughborough was a rewarding corridor to exercise a Day Anywhere ticket, with other operators to be seen en route and at the destination. BMMO and Trent co-ordinated its activities and one of the latter's Leyland Atlanteans can be seen in this view of St Margaret's. Sandacre D9 5330 is closest to the camera, then a DD11 Fleetline, a D7, the LD8 is a rarity for the Leicester area, and finally a 1962 S15. In 1967 the daily tally of Midland Red departures from St Margaret's was 406 Sandacre buses, 163 Southgate Street, 90 Wigston and 47 Coalville vehicles. Trent accounted for a further 48. The original concrete shelters of St Margaret's Bus Station were perhaps photogenic in a Bauhaus sort of way as they aged; the terminal was extensively rebuilt in the mid-1980s to excellent effect. *T C Bassindale/ The Transport Museum, Wythall*

LEFT 101 was Midland Red's first Leyland National and delivered before imposition of NBC poppy red and lettering. It spent most of its early years at Southgate Street but did have two months at Sandacre as seen here on 14 July 1974 when it was carrying advertisement colours somewhat reminiscent of West Midlands PTE! It moved to Wigston in May 1980. *Malcolm Keeley*

LEICESTER WIGSTON

Opened: 5 October 1957

To Midland Red East 6 September 1981; relaunched as Midland Fox January 1984, relaunched as Arriva 1997

Still in use

By the mid-1950s the two existing Leicester garages were seriously overcrowded so the opening of this garage, on Station Street, South Wigston, four miles south of the city centre, was much needed. It was designed for 65 vehicles but there was room for outdoor parking at the rear. The additional garage relieved both Southgate Street and Sandacre Street, twenty buses initially being transferred from each. Wigston took over services to the south-east of the city. All the received routes were from Southgate Street, its buses sharing the SS blind code until receiving their own WS for Wigston blinds in 1960, so a number of services passed from Sandacre to Southgate Street. Wigston's spacious dock area performed the centralised dock function for buses from the eastern area garages.

The poverty of latterday Midland Red deprived the Leicester area of vital double-deckers. When Midland Fox allocated five Olympians to Wigston in November 1989, these were the garage's first brand new double-deck buses since Fleetlines 6206-7 were delivered twenty years earlier!

BELOW Front elevation of Wigston garage. *BMMO*

RIGHT Wigston's spacious dock area upon opening of the garage. Beyond the two D7s is an ex-Kemp & Shaw Guy over one of the pits. *BMMO*

BELOW RIGHT Buses parked in the yard on 4 March 1979 include, on the right, S23 5941 which was the very last bus totally constructed at Carlyle Works, entering service in January 1970. S23s 5942-91 had their bodies completed by Plaxton. *David Barber*

LICHFIELD

Opened: 17 September 1954
Closed: 28 May 1971

Perhaps as a reflection of post-war optimism, this was a big site on Trent Valley Road that, in the event, was not all required. The garage had a capacity of 30 vehicles, originally taking work from Tamworth, Sutton Coldfield and Stafford garages. It is possible that the provision of a garage here was to mitigate staff shortages elsewhere, particularly the last two towns mentioned, but the allocation peaked at only 19 in 1960. The brick constructed garage included an Enquiry Office (although another could be found in the centre of the city) and had entrances at the side and rear where there was a large amount of unsurfaced land, presumably in the hope of further expansion. The boom times were over, however, and Lichfield's spare space became famous to Midland Red enthusiasts as the last resting place of most buses awaiting sale to and collection by the scrapman.

The garage contributed to important routes 112 (Birmingham – Burton), 765 to Tamworth and Coventry and 825 to Stafford; these three keeping nine Lichfield buses fully occupied. Other routes connected the cathedral city of three spires with local villages and there were works services to Rugeley and Stafford. The 112 meant there were always some dual-purpose buses among the allocation of mainly BMMO types.

With the premises seriously underused and Sutton Coldfield continuing to suffer its staffing shortages, some work was transferred to Lichfield from 4 October 1969, reintroducing double-deckers after a brief period without them. These worked the S67/76 Erdington-New Oscott-Parson & Clerk services but Midland Red abandoned them in February 1971; West Midlands PTE picking up some of the pieces. Lichfield garage closed soon after and its work widely spread. The building still stands at the time of writing.

ABOVE The interior of Lichfield garage when new. The garage was built by J R Deacon of Lichfield with the steel frame and roof cladding supplied by T Partridge and Co Ltd, Darlaston. The ability to totally enclose the docking area with partitions was noteworthy at the time. S8 3264 and D5 3554, transferred from Tamworth and Stafford, receive attention over the inspection pits. *BMMO*

BELOW The garage viewed from Trent Valley Road, then the main A38 to Burton and Derby. The side entrance, somewhat overrun by cars including a Reliant built in nearby Tamworth, led to the garage and the large area of land at the back. *Ken Jubb*

ABOVE RIGHT Ex-Kemp & Shaw 1949 Barnards-bodied Guy spent nearly two years working from Lichfield in 1959-61 and is seen here receiving minor attention in the garage. *Ken Jubb*

RIGHT 1938-9 FEDDs on the withdrawn vehicles dump at the back of the garage. 2373 (FHA 877) and 2140 (EHA 272) stand either side of 2158 (EHA 290) – the wider cab of the middle bus is not an illusion as it was one of three that originally entered service with full width cabs and rebuilt later. *Ken Jubb*

LUDLOW

Opened: 1 January 1951
To Midland Red North 6 September 1981
Closed: 20 May 1983. Yard retained as outstation until April 1987

Midland Red buses worked the border country between England and Wales, and visitors have long been attracted to this jewel of a town, now known not just for its castle and picturesque old buildings but as a gourmet centre. The tiny 12-bus garage in Weeping Cross Lane was the first new BMMO garage to be built after World War Two and, while its appearance did not equal the Feathers Hotel in the town or many other Midland Red garages, proud staff maintained rock gardens on the frontage. The single bay steel framed structure had a prefabricated exterior and the roof glazing introduced 'Perspex' to the company's properties. Land alongside permitted outdoor parking for more vehicles.

The X34/35 (later 434/5) Shrewsbury – Ludlow - Hereford services were a major responsibility for Ludlow, being largely but not exclusively operated by this garage. There were several rural services, including routes 971-3 to Bridgnorth and beyond (taken over from Corvedale of Ludlow on 2 May 1953), Kidderminster to Tenbury, and from Leominster to Bromyard and Presteigne. Another shared service was the 192 to Birmingham (later X92). Daily journeys on the 192 commenced on 20 May 1950, before the garage opened, using double-deck buses from the start. A Sunday service had been operated since 15 May 1932, later joined by Saturday journeys. The route involved some hard climbs and dangerous corners; over Clee Hill the road is 1,249 feet above sea level although the summit of the hill is 500 feet higher. This stretch is obviously more prone to fog, frost, ice and snow but the view from a double-decker on a fine day was majestic.

Drivers at, say, Hartshill probably dreamed of their Ludlow compatriots serving the likes of Church Stretton and Cleobury Mortimer, travelling all day over sun-filled highways through rich, fertile countryside or along Wenlock Edge – a view of Clee Hill or an ancient castle over your shoulder. None of these places had heavy peak demands, however, so Ludlow's older buses did not have much opportunity to lounge alongside the garage between the peaks, unlike many other places. In fact, Ludlow's buses incurred the highest daily mileages in the fleet.

AD2s on the opening allocation were not ideal for Ludlow's operations which suited buses with doors. They were soon replaced by D5Bs but the powerful LD8s that followed were even better on the open roads to Birmingham, Hereford and Shrewsbury. Single-deck types associated with Ludlow are S14s and Leopards. The garage became all single-deck from 1964 but Fleetlines were later allocated.

Ludlow was included in the largely Shrewsbury-based 'Hotspur' network, introduced on 24 November 1979. The 434/5 were withdrawn, the southern ends being replaced by extending the X92 to Hereford and by the 953 respectively, while north of Ludlow was superseded by the 955/6. Midland Red North and West operated the X92 jointly after the 1981 split. Upon Ludlow's closure by North, the X92 became entirely operated by West from 20 May 1983, the latter also taking over dual-purpose Leopard/ Plaxtons 460/5/6/8 with the increased responsibilities.

Part of the frontage was taken for road widening in 1967 while, the following year, part of the yard reverted to the original owner for expansion of the timber business. The garage still exists but the yard is now occupied by a retail unit.

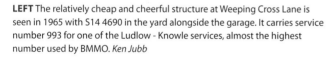

LEFT The relatively cheap and cheerful structure at Weeping Cross Lane is seen in 1965 with S14 4690 in the yard alongside the garage. It carries service number 993 for one of the Ludlow - Knowle services, almost the highest number used by BMMO. *Ken Jubb*

TOP The X34/5 Shrewsbury-Ludlow-Hereford was a wonderful route to ride on a double-decker. Travel north of Ludlow along the hilly A49, past the ancient medieval fortified mansion, Stokesay Castle, and you reach the three Strettons – Little Stretton, Church Stretton and All Stretton. The middle of these drew huge crowds on fine days with the great ridge of the Long Mynd to the west, nearly 1,700 feet high, and lovely Carding Mill Valley. In the 1950s summers, the double-decker fleet at Ludlow was boosted by the transfer for the season of three double-deckers from Bearwood, with a fourth if necessary at the peak. The X34/35 were converted to 36 feet long single-deckers from May 1964 when Ludlow lost its double-deck fleet. The X prefix became exclusively used for limited stop services so the X34/5 services were renumbered 434/5 in 1966. The following year some journeys were rerouted via Condover and Ryton, permitting economies on the 956/7. BMMO S17 5484 prepares to cross Ludford bridge in 1969 with a splendid view back towards the town. *Ken Jubb*

ABOVE LEFT Willowbrook-bodied Leyland Leopard 6408 briefly worked from Ludlow garage when new in August 1971 and is seen leaving Shrewsbury. *Ken Jubb*

ABOVE Midland Red ran from Leominster to Presteigne, the latter although located east of Offa's Dyke nevertheless just inside Wales, in traditional Radnorshire and nowadays in the county of Powys. This was an infrequent service but deeply rural bus travel was perhaps easier than may be thought today. At Leominster there were hourly buses to Hereford, Ludlow and Shrewsbury. Key journeys on the Presteigne service were timed to connect with the similarly infrequent 422 to and from Bromyard where passengers could make a further timetabled connection with the 420 to and from Worcester. The 4xx service number betrays that this service originally operated from Hereford. There was also the important local independent operator, G D Bengry, trading as Primrose Motor Services, one of whose vehicles is in the background here at Leominster in early 1971. Ludlow was one of the garages that had Ford/ Plaxton demonstrator GTW 185H on trial, leading to substantial orders. New Midland Red Ford/ Plaxton 6376 is collecting a layer of dirt from the country roads and will not look pristine in Presteigne. *Ken Jubb*

MALVERN PORTLAND ROAD

Opened: January 1930
Closed: 15 August 1954

The Malverns comprise seven settlements with Malvern in their names. Nearly all Worcestershire Motor Transport's buses were almost immediately commandeered by the military for World War One and BMMO took over complete operation from 1 November 1914. BMMO then began to develop its network of bus services and, later, tours in and around Malvern. The Malvern local services of W & B Woodyatt Ltd were taken over in 1916.

The opening of the garage, leased from Woodyatt in Portland Road, Great Malvern, eliminated wasteful mileage from Worcester but it was uncomfortably sited on a bend. It was an old red brick structure with corrugated iron roof surmounted by a long glazed clerestory. It operated as a separate garage for traffic staff but engineering was handled by Worcester as the vehicle capacity was only about eight, with the possibility of around three more parked outside. Only single-deck buses ran from here, carrying Worcester codes, and CHA-registered SONs were a familiar sight. Malvern's local services were renumbered into an M prefixed series from 7 January 1935.

The old Portland Road premises seen in 1960, six years after its replacement. *Ken Jubb*

MALVERN SPRING LANE

Opened: 16 August 1954
Closed: 1 October 1976

The new garage in Spring Lane, Malvern Link, became operational in August 1954 and officially opened on 10 September. It was the first company garage to be built with tubular roof trusses instead of the usual girder construction but still looked a typical, handsome BMMO property, further benefiting from its attractive siting. It was of single bay construction with entrance/exits and forecourts at both ends. The new Malvern garage was capable of holding 33 buses and thus well able to cope with the expansion of the town and take some pressure off Worcester. The opening allocation of 21 included ex-Portland Road SONs. Fifteen local services plus some works and school services were worked at the outset, together with country services – some Worcester-based. The small allocation of double-deck buses formed the garage's new share of the 144 route to Birmingham. The rest of the allocation was entirely single-deck, even these were a tight fit through Abbey Gateway, extensively used by Malvern town services until traffic was banned.

In view of the limited amount of heavy urban work here, it is surprising that Malvern proved to be the last garage to introduce any one-man operated workings on 2 May 1970. This restricted the number of modern vehicles so, at that date, it could still boast an entirely BMMO allocation although this soon changed with some Leopard coaches and saloons.

BMMO buses were still numerous when the Spring Lane garage closed. The local network was revised, with the M prefix no longer being used, and work reverted to Worcester garage. An echo of the old days came with the revival of the M prefix under yet another revised service pattern introduced with 'Severnlink' branding from 13 January 1979, only to lose it again from March 1982. The garage has been demolished.

Malvern Thrills

The 144 Birmingham-Worcester service ran for many decades beyond Worcester to Malvern Wells and was worked by Digbeth, Worcester, Bromsgrove and Malvern garages. The Malvern Wells terminus, set high in the hills, had a turning circle with sufficient depth to accommodate buses like FEDDs and D7s in one swing but D9s and Fleetlines were too long so a reverse across the main road was virtually inevitable. One night a 36-feet long S16 helping out was part way through its multi-point turn when the lever of the manual gearbox snapped off with the bus stuck across the road.

Lloyd Penfold remembers the day a Digbeth D9 broke down at the 144 terminus. A Malvern mechanic came to the rescue in another D9, found that he had not got the part required and telephoned for another mechanic to bring it out. He came in a D9 too. By this time the next service bus had arrived (yet another D9 but from Worcester garage). Its driver stopped the bus up the road and walked down to see what the trouble was. When he returned to his D9 it wouldn't start – the batteries were flat. At this point a little old lady saw four buses instead of the usual one and asked a conductor which was first. "None of these" was the weary reply.

ABOVE The rounded façade of the garage disguised the roof design of tubular trusses supporting asbestos and Perspex roof panels. 1962 S15 5077 completes a view of the bus garage, altogether presenting a perfect image to the travelling public in Spring 1966. Buses entered the garage at the other end of the building. The M13 was a circular introduced on 26 June 1965 upon a reorganisation of Malvern's local services. *Ken Jubb*

RIGHT 1963 D9 5341 receives attention at the garage on 30 May 1976. *Garry Yates*

MARKFIELD

Taken over from Brown's Blue Coaches 16 March 1963
Closed: 30 June 1968

D7 4407 returns to Markfield garage just before its closure. *Ken Jubb*

Brown's Blue had more than one premises but only this garage with access from Little Shaw Lane and Stanton Lane was taken over with the business. It was built as a bus garage in 1935 and consisted of three separate buildings next to each other of varying sizes, all steel framed with corrugated iron cladding, plus a large unsurfaced forecourt. Around 15 vehicles were kept here but Midland Red did not purchase any of the Brown's Blue stock, the work being covered by buses drafted in from other garages. Although

Markfield had its own allocation of vehicles it was regarded as a sub-depot of Coalville and shared the CE code. It was mostly associated with D7s in its brief Midland Red era but did operate other types, surviving long enough to receive a few new buses such as S17 5492 and D9s 5315/34/57. The vehicles and services passed upon closure to Coalville and the garage sold for further use later in 1968.

NUNEATON COTON ROAD

Opened: 21 December 1921
Closed: May 1960

A sister BET company, the North Warwickshire Motor Omnibus & Traction Company, Ltd., got into difficulties during World War I and, from 1 February 1918, Midland Red buses started to work what remained of its network of services out of Nuneaton and Twogates, near Tamworth.

This purpose-built garage replaced the ex-North Warwickshire garage in Burgage Walk, used since June 1917, and also rented premises in Heath End Road. BMMO had to overcome a lot of opposition buses but the new red brick three-bay steel-framed garage soon needed extending in 1923 and again in 1925, in both events by adding further bays of almost identical style, increasing capacity to 50. The linked office building included a Booking and Enquiry Office.

Nuneaton garage was built too early to have considered the operation of closed-top double-deckers. 1920 Garfords could be found here, otherwise it was the usual range of single-deck types from Tilling-Stevens TS3s onwards, with SOS IM4s and BMMO S6s and S14s particularly numerous.

Service numbers 725-775 were allocated to Nuneaton under the 1928 renumbering and the N prefix was first employed for local services on 9 May 1932. Coal had encouraged numerous industries, including textiles, and Nuneaton's duties included a number of colliery services. Residents working in the car factories of Coventry created another important demand. Breaking into all this urban mileage was a share in the 765 Coventry – Nuneaton – Tamworth – Lichfield route and a few other infrequent rural services.

A view of the Coton Road garage with its five-gabled frontage in April 1960, immediately before replacement. The later bays are at the far end. Nearest to the camera is a property purchased from the Nuneaton Ex-Service Men's Club in February 1942. *Ken Jubb*

The former picture house forming the Nuneaton Motor Company's Empire garage on 4 June 1932. The bus entrance is on the extreme right. *BMMO*

Coton Road was briefly supplemented by part of a former theatre and public house, latterly the Nuneaton Motor Company's Empire garage, rented to house around a dozen vehicles between June 1932 and 31 December 1934 – the arrangement ceasing with the opening of Hinckley garage.

In 1955 the garage claimed the company's tallest driver (over 6 feet 9 inches), the shortest conductress (4 feet 9 inches), the heaviest employee (only 24 stones, having got his weight down from 29), and an unnamed heaviest conductress weighing in at 16 stone 10 pounds.

Nuneaton Borough Council first advised in 1945 that Coton Road was in the way of road improvements; the post-war travel boom soon underlined the company's need for a larger garage. An early proposal from the Borough Council was a combined garage and bus station in Harefield Road. The company advised that the site was not big enough for both so a spacious 'Central Omnibus Station' was constructed there and opened in May 1956. The council offered a new site off Newtown Road, conveniently close to the bus station, and the replacement bus garage opened in May 1960; the Coton Road premises being demolished soon after closure.

NUNEATON NEWTOWN ROAD

Opened: 9 May 1960 (official opening 1 June 1960)
To Midland Red South 6 September 1981, to Stagecoach December 1993
Still in use

The replacement premises for Coton Road had the elements of the Midland Red post-war style with extensive offices either side of the entrance but the large brick façade over the latter was rather overpowering. A side driveway led to a large rear parking yard with vehicle access into the garage which could hold 77 buses. The previous premises had not been capable of accommodating covered-top double-deck buses but the new garage was not restricted, however, and Daimler Fleetlines, along with Leopard saloons, soon joined the BMMO types. A Midland Red Enquiry Office and Travel Bureau could be found at both the new garage and the modern bus station, the latter in a shop rented from the council.

Nuneaton garage supplied the motorway coaches for the London-Coventry service, logically soon extended to and from Nuneaton, a good example of the company ensuring outer garages enjoyed some premier work. The local identity name of 'Hunter' was introduced on 12 May 1979, the accompanying MAP scheme causing the closure of nearby Hinckley garage. Minibus operations began here on 27 October 1986.

The Newtown Road garage at the time of its opening in 1960. This end looks much the same today apart from the addition of a fire escape to the right of the vehicle door and, of course, later owners have changed the branding. *BMMO*

ABOVE A confusing via point for Brummies as 1950 Brush-bodied S10 3727 works a Nuneaton local service from the 'Central Omnibus Station' on 27 July 1963. This Bull Ring is towards Coton. *Alan D Broughall*

BELOW Driver tuition vehicles were based at Nuneaton for many years. Two members of the Midland Red South training fleet seen in the yard were ORF 458F, an ex-Harpers 1968 Leyland Leopard with Duple Northern body with most of a Plaxton dash panel grafted on, and 552 OHU, a 1963 Bristol FLF from Bristol Omnibus. Manual gearbox buses were favoured for tuition buses to give the driver a good working over and, if required, an all-types licence, so the Harpers' Leopard was preferred to one of Midland Red's own which were all semi-automatics. *Ian Thomas/ The Transport Museum, Wythall*

An early post-war view of Oldbury garage with its clock tower topped by a flag pole. *BMMO*

OLDBURY

Opened: 12 April 1937
To West Midlands Passenger Transport Executive 3 December 1973
Closed: 25 January 1986

Oldbury was in the northern tip of Worcestershire before local government reorganisation in 1974 and the town was known worldwide for its industries, particularly tubes and chemicals. Its Midland Red garage occupied a prominent corner site at Birchley Crossing on the Wolverhampton New Road. It had a very distinctive, even futuristic, looking frontage. A slender clock tower surmounted a flat-roofed office block that stood forward on a peninsula ahead of the two garage bays. The block included a round fronted Booking and Enquiry Office and made a considerable architectural statement at this important road crossing. The clock tower took a battering from the weather and was removed in 1968.

The official opening capacity of 70 vehicles was justified when the last tramways in the Black Country were replaced by motorbuses from 1 October 1939, despite the outbreak of World War Two the previous month. This last conversion involved the routes from central Birmingham along the Dudley Road to Bearwood, Soho, and through Oldbury to Dudley. By then the entire group was being operated by Birmingham City Transport tramcars on behalf of the local

authorities along the route. Those outside Birmingham – Smethwick, Oldbury, Rowley Regis and Tipton – made agreements that Midland Red should operate the replacing buses on their behalves. The replacement bus services were thus theoretically jointly operated, in some cases fortunately reusing the tram numbers, but with Midland Red B for Birmingham local service prefixes. Basically, Birmingham City Transport ran the B80-83 to Bearwood, Soho and short workings, while Midland Red ran the B84-89 beyond to Smethwick, Oldbury and Dudley, although there were exceptions to balance the mileage between BCT and BMMO. The B80-89 became 80-89 from 30 June 1968 upon a request from BCT which closed its Rosebery Street garage on that date, resulting in Midland Red having service numbers below 100 for the first time since 1925.

Most of the final batch of FEDDs, FHA 836-85, were allocated to garages providing the tram replacement services, Oldbury receiving no less than 35, one of the largest single allocations of one batch of buses, and six to Dudley. The FEDD predominance was dented in 1942 when

105

they were joined by the nine Leyland TD7s, transferred to Wolverhampton in 1949. Non-BMMO types didn't seem to thrive at Oldbury until the Fleetline era – AD2s and LD8s were soon moved on.

In addition to the tram replacement route, known as 'The Track', Oldbury had a share in the Wolverhampton New Road services and also operated a range of urban services from Birmingham and Bearwood through Langley and Oldbury, some continuing to destinations beyond.

Oldbury was the first BMMO garage to have an automatic bus washer, manufactured by Essex. Another first for Oldbury was the introduction of differential running time from 6 September 1969. Reduced running time was applied to evening and Sunday journeys on the section of route outside Birmingham on the 86/87 – Dudley to Windmill Lane being reduced from 31 to 24 minutes.

In PTE days, Oldbury became particularly associated with Volvo Ailsas. Upon closure the work was transferred to Dudley and the ex-municipal bus garage at West Bromwich. Oldbury garage was subsequently demolished.

LEFT Midland Red's first true wartime deliveries were nine Leyland Titan TD7 models received in 1942. Nos 2432-7 had Duple bodies to full wartime angular specification while 2438-40 were bodied by Northern Counties with metal frames and were comparatively robust. They initially ran from Oldbury but were transferred to Wolverhampton in 1949. The Duple bodies were heavily rebuilt in 1951, including facelifting to disguise the worst of the wartime austerity features. This was not the end of the changes as all nine received BMMO engines in 1952-3. 2437 is parked on the forecourt of Oldbury after its body had been rebuilt by Carlyle Works. The TD7s were taken out of service in 1954-5. *Barry Ware*

BELOW A good view of the style of cast company name erected on properties built in the 1930s. The single-deck allocation at Oldbury was fairly small. The first production run of single-deckers with power doors was the S13 class, mostly built in 1952 to dual-purpose specification. The year of this view is 1966 and S13 3949 is now simply regarded as a bus, hence the all-red livery. *Ken Jubb*

REDDITCH CHURCH ROAD

Opened: 1 July 1931
To Midland Red West 6 September 1981, relaunched as First in November 2001
Closed: 21 January 2004

When the garage opened, Redditch was much smaller than today. The new garage in Church Road was in the ornamental red brick style but smaller than usual, having capacity for 25 buses, increased to 35 with an extension at one end, built in 1938. The town's Drill Hall was around the corner, backing onto the garage, and this was conveyed to the company in 1962. Internal walls were removed and non-vehicular access provided to the existing garage, buses being parked in the former Drill Hall from 1965.

The garage handled important services to Birmingham, Bromsgrove, Evesham and Worcester via Inkberrow. First use of the R prefix was from 14 May 1934 with more following from 1 October. The 1928 service renumbering had allocated 318-351 to Bromsgrove and Redditch but the former had taken the lion's share. In consequence, some R services went rather further than Midland Red locals in other towns. Redditch was never a garage associated with non-BMMO types, BHA FEDDs and D5Bs were familiar here for years.

The travel to work data in the 1966 Census showed large flows between Redditch and the West Midlands conurbation and this further increased as the town was massively enlarged as Birmingham overspill. Redditch was therefore included in the original West Midlands Passenger Transport Executive area. Relatively slow progress was made on an operating agreement between WMPTE and Midland Red. By the

TOP Church Road garage in 1969. *Ken Jubb*

ABOVE 1936 Metro-Cammell bodied FEDD 1840, converted to diesel with a BMMO K engine in 1945, stands outside Redditch garage. The registration of this bus, BHA 399, is recalled in BHA 399C (bus 5399), the D9 on the back cover and now preserved at Wythall. *R A Mills/ The Transport Museum, Wythall*

107

time it was settled, it was known that a new West Midlands County was on its way and, as the boundaries of that were not determined on transport movements, Redditch was not included in it. The town's garage thus stayed with Midland Red and, in March 1976, was the first recipient of local branding – 'Reddibus' and its 'Redditickets' was probably the most appropriate brand name of them all! The success of Reddibus led to improvements from 27 October 1979. This included the introduction of the R19, linking Redditch to Solihull for the first time, travelling via Tanworth-in-Arden. The 'Reddibus'

brand survived in use until 19 April 1986 when most town services were converted to Mercedes-Benz minibuses with 'Reddilink' branding.

The Church Road garage was retained after the opening of Plymouth Road in 1978 to handle the heavier maintenance of the town's buses but lost its Traffic functions. It was sold to a property developer after its closure in 2004, the maintenance responsibilities having passed to Kidderminster and Worcester. It has since enjoyed periods under lease to other bus operators.

LEFT The 339 was an infrequent route from Bromsgrove and Redditch to Stratford, worked on 25 May 1963 by 1952 Brush-bodied S13 3899. Travellers for Midland Red and Stratford Blue country services linger around 3899 in the Red Lion bus station at Stratford. *Andrew Willis*

BELOW Inside the garage in July 1958 are two 1951 D5Bs parked on full lock with 1939 FEDD 2255 also prominent. Brush built the 56-seat bodies on all three. *F W York/ The Transport Museum, Wythall*

TOP RIGHT S10 3655 was an engineering float vehicle that spent some time at Redditch garage in 1966. *Ken Jubb*

ABOVE The one-a-day in each direction 347 Birmingham – Ullenhall – Alcester service was deleted after 4 November 1966 and the R13 between Redditch and Ullenhall was introduced the following day. Despite the impression given by the local service number, even today Ullenhall and Beoley remain small villages well outside Redditch. The R13 generally ran twice a day and took 35 minutes in each direction; S16 5525 is seen in 1971. Redditch's first bus station was opened on 9 May 1953 and Ministry-imposed financial rules of the time meant it had to be constructed as cheaply as possible, shelters rendered surplus in the town being re-erected here. *Ken Jubb*

LEFT Construction of the new town included routes specifically for public transport. Among the Reddibus success stories was the R15 which began with ex-London Country Ford Transits such as 443 (XPE 123N) and soon needed the Ford/ Plaxton 45-seat buses shortened to 27-seat midibuses by the company. 45-seaters were introduced from 27 October 1979, the midibuses being transferred to new services. *Malcolm Keeley*

REDDITCH PLYMOUTH ROAD

Opened: 10 June 1978

To Midland Red West 6 September 1981, relaunched as First in November 2001. Sold to Diamond Bus 3 March 2013

Still in use

This new parking area with servicing bay and wash was opened adjacent to the Transport Interchange along the closed Redditch – Evesham railway line. All Redditch buses operated from this new site and the additional capacity enabled the use of Evesham-allocated buses on Redditch local services to cease.

Diamond Bus purchased vehicles and the garages at Redditch and Kidderminster – the latter premises being the replacement for the ex-Midland Red garage.

The new Transport Interchange directly connected to the Kingfisher shopping centre was opened in 1973. Leyland Nationals 484-9 were delivered new to Redditch for the service relaunch on 13 March 1976 and remained there for many years. No 487 is seen at the bus station on 7 November 1981; the style of branding remained unique to Reddibus. *Malcolm Keeley*

Reddibus

COMPLETE SERVICE —
BIRMINGHAM — ALVECHURCH —
REDDITCH, INCLUDING LIMITED
STOP SERVICES X5, X6 and X7 AND
STOPPING SERVICE 146

R7 Redditch Astwood Bank Cookhill

147 Birmingham Alvechurch Redditch Astwood Bank Cookhill

November 1978

ABOVE At first glance looking like one of Midland Red's indigenous Fords, 2181 (XUX 417K) was a 1972 Plaxton 47-seat bodied R192 acquired when the Oakengates – Dawley service of Hoggins, Wrockwardine Wood, was taken over on 7 January 1974. It briefly joined the Redditch allocation in 1978 before withdrawal from service and is seen on the Plymouth Road parking area on 23 February 1979. *E V Trigg*

RIGHT Bend it like busmen. After a decade of standard National Bus Company vehicles, the five hired MAN articulated buses were an amazing contrast. They were not repainted from their South Yorkshire PTE days and retained fleet numbers 2001-5. Nos 2004 and 2001 load at the Transport Interchange for Crabbs Cross and Matchborough respectively on 28 March 1983. *Malcolm Keeley*

RIGHT Deregulation led to competition from double-deck buses operated on the Matchborough Circular by Redline, owned by ex-Midland Red West employees. MRW answered from October 1987 by hiring Bristol VRT/ ECW two-door buses from sister company Bristol Omnibus. Three were soon purchased in April 1988, 5031-2 dating from 1975 and 5039 from 1976, and ran until 1990. This 23 April 1988 view at the Transport Interchange shows 5039 (JHW 113P) in the livery of its previous operator with the Midland Red West triangular wyvern logo added on the front and the fleetname above the rear wheels. Behind is an ex-Alder Valley Bristol VRT of Redline. *Malcolm Keeley*

RUGBY

Opened: 9 March 1926
To Midland Red South 6 September 1981, to Stagecoach December 1993
Still in use

In addition to an arguably inappropriate image of toffs playing with odd-shaped balls, Rugby found fame as a railway centre while the large works of electrical giants BTH and English Electric provided employment for Midland Red buses. Leamington-based buses served Rugby from the early 1920s but the town quickly got its own garage. This was initially a dormitory shed of Leamington but soon got engineering facilities and its own allocation of vehicles. This original steel frame garage in Railway Terrace, holding around a dozen buses, had brick and panelled exterior with a large curved roof of corrugated sheeting. A tiny brick office stood alongside. These premises soon proved inadequate and, from November 1929, five or six buses were housed down the road at Dawson's Garage.

Land was purchased from the London Midland & Scottish Railway Co in 1932 allowing new premises also in Railway Terrace to be built, opening on 8 November 1934 and replacing the existing arrangements. The long single-bay steel frame building was clad in metal or asbestos sheeting, probably to speed construction, and held 30 buses. Extensions completed in May 1938 and January 1942 increased capacity to 54.

The 1928 service renumbering reserved 576-600 for Rugby but, in practice, numbers 570-97 were seen in the town. In addition to services looking towards Coventry, the garage operated country services to destinations like Daventry, Lutterworth and Market Harborough. Also important were the local services; the prefix letter R was introduced here on 7

January 1935. Rugby also contributed to the long X96 between Northampton and Shrewsbury. Earlier types associated with the garage were IMs and S8s. A celebrity vehicle here for many years was the S2 underfloor-engine prototype no 1942.

Adjoining land was purchased from the British Transport Commission in 1954. The existing garage was transformed into a largely new building opened in March 1967 after two years' work, able to accommodate 73 vehicles of 36-feet length and, at last, double-deckers – a batch of new Fleetlines, 6061-6, was soon allocated here. Services between Coventry and Rugby were revised on 7 October 1967 with use of double-deckers where practicable. An Enquiry Office was included in the corner office block of the new garage. Rugby is still going strong and nowadays includes Stagecoach Megabus work among its duties.

FAR LEFT The original garage in Railway Terrace. This was soon filled, necessitating the hiring of nearby premises. *BMMO*

BELOW LEFT The 1934 garage in Railway Terrace seen after World War Two. As hinted by the address, the Midland Red garage was opposite the main line railway station. The company name was therefore liberally applied in large letters to ensure the attention of passengers travelling aboard the opposition! *PM Photography*

BELOW A view around the corner in Railway Approach, directly facing the railway station, showing the new exit created in the 1967 building. *BMMO*

BOTTOM A lucky shot showing two of the three 1948-9 S8s fitted with S15 fronts and improved interiors in 1957-8. 3217 is leading 3237, both on local services. *Ken Jubb*

ABOVE Ford/ Plaxton 6316 wearing poppy red in the garage on 30 May 1976. *Garry Yates*

RIGHT Vehicles of several hues, but not a lot of red, block the entrance to Rugby garage on 9 July 1997. Stagecoach drafted in buses from other subsidiaries – the blue double-decker was 991 (MVK 558R), one of several rather fine Alexander-bodied Leyland Atlanteans new to Tyne and Wear PTE. Others were in Tyne and Wear yellow and white or Stagecoach's own livery, represented here by a secondhand Bristol VRT. *Malcolm Keeley*

SHREWSBURY

Opened: 11 November 1920

To Midland Red North 6 September 1981, relaunched as Arriva 1997

Closed: 5 June 2012

The broad River Severn almost encircles this fine town set in a predominantly rural county and buses operate through narrow and hilly streets amongst a picturesque treasure house of 16th/17th century Tudor and Elizabethan architecture. The Allen Omnibus Company Ltd. of London had a one-bus operation at Shrewsbury. This became an isolated outpost of BMMO after the company took over from 1 April 1916 and was literally a cowboy operation as its employee Mr J Davis had been formerly employed on a ranch in the Argentine. This lone ranger had to drive, clean, inspect and maintain his bus and he eventually became Shrewsbury's Engineering Foreman and Resident Engineer.

RIGHT Harry Trigg of Bearwood garage is helping to establish Midland Red facilities from Shrewsbury where the services were initially separated from the rest of the network. OH 1216 was a 1920 Tilling-Stevens TS3. *E V Trigg*

BELOW Shrewsbury garage being extended in December 1929 with SOS QL HA 4815 parked in one of the existing entrances.
The Transport Museum, Wythall collection

BMMO also took over the tenancy of the ex-Allen garage in Abbey Foregate, which had to be vacated before purpose-built premises in Ditherington were completed. By then there was a handful of buses to be moved to a large shed leased in Roushill, opening on 1 July 1919.

The steel framed red brick garage in Ditherington opened in 1920 had capacity for fifteen buses. There were originally only two broad entrances on the frontage, this arrangement being neatly repeated almost exactly in a major extension built in 1929. Extra office accommodation was provided in 1930.

Most of the garage was requisitioned for aircraft production during World War Two, forcing the company to use additional, rather less suitable, premises between 25 November 1940 and 28 February 1946. This was a flood-prone shed near Abbey Foregate at Old Coleham.

By 1935 the garage had capacity for 53 buses but this became insufficient in the early post-war years. Buses had to be parked on the forecourt until adjacent land was purchased in 1948. This enabled some open parking and also released space in the garage to create facilities to carry out minor body overhauls for Shrewsbury vehicles and other nearby garages.

The 1928 renumbering allocated all the numbers above 926 to the Shrewsbury area although a few were later stolen for Ludlow services. The S prefix letter for local services was introduced on 11 June 1934. Ditherington has had mainly a single-deck allocation, including dual-purpose buses for the X96 to Northampton. In addition to the many local services,

the garage also contributed to the X34/35 to Hereford and other services down the same corridor to Church Stretton and Ludlow. Other country services included Wellington, Market Drayton, Bridgnorth, Oswestry, Ellesmere, Whitchurch (joint with Salopia), and Wem. Services to the south-east of the town passed the 132 feet high pillar known locally as 'The Column', said to be the tallest Doric pillar in the world. It is only 13 feet shorter than the (non-Doric) Nelson Column in Trafalgar Square. On top is General Lord Rowland Hill – with the Duke of Wellington at the Battle of Waterloo and no relation to Sir Rowland Hill, founder of the penny post celebrated in Kidderminster as a former resident.

Double-deckers arrived after World War Two and were mainly AD2s in the early days. Other non-BMMOs prior to the 1970s were LS18s.

'Hotspur' was the local identity introduced on 24 November 1979, recalling the Yorkist champion, Sir Henry Percy – otherwise known as Harry Hotspur – who was killed at the Battle of Shrewsbury in 1403. The revised network tried to reduce the delays caused by traffic congestion. 'Hotspur' was shared by Ludlow and Wellington garages.

Ditherington's replacement at Harlescott opened on 3 June 2012, the buses for the ordinary services having been delivered to the new premises after their work the previous evening. Ditherington closed on 5 June when the park and ride vehicles ran in to Harlescott after service. The old garage was demolished soon after.

LEFT The garage as it looked on 10 April 1994.
Garry Yates

ABOVE 1940 SON 2420 is seen in the yard alongside the garage in Ditherington. Midland Red did not indulge in many body exchanges after the very early days but 2420's original was replaced by one heavily rebuilt with flush-mounted windows and sliding vents by Nudd Bros, removed from 2409, withdrawn at the end of November 1955. 2420, remaining at Shrewsbury, was eventually one of the last pair of SONs in passenger service (the other was engineering floater 2425), both retiring at the end of October 1958. Dominating the background is Flax Mill, built in 1796-7; the oldest iron framed building in the world and regarded as the grandfather of the skyscraper. It is a Grade 1 listed building, internationally important and demolishing the bus garage was seen as a vital part of regenerating the Flax Mill and its surroundings. *T W W Knowles*

ABOVE RIGHT The large bus station, including a Midland Red enquiry office, in Barker Street was opened on 13 January 1952 and the company had exclusive use of it from Shrewsbury council. The station was filled with Midland Red buses travelling near and far - S9 3378 and S14 4275 are working locals, the latter is travelling to the site of the Battle of Shrewsbury. *The Transport Museum, Wythall*

RIGHT The two ex-Kemp & Shaw Guy Arab IIIs with rare Barnards 35-seat bodies, new in April 1949, survived until the spring of 1962, a remarkably long time bearing in mind the rest of the Midland Red single-deck fleet was by then underfloor-engined. They moved from Leicester fairly quickly for new pastures within Midland Red. After a couple of months at Ludlow, 4842 was a surprising addition to Shrewsbury's allocation from September 1959, and remained there until retirement. *The Transport Museum, Wythall*

ABOVE The early 16th century timbered mansion, Rowley's House, provided a superb photographic backdrop to Barker Street and new S17s 5683 and 5684 are on view here in 1966. The buses were removed in 1989 to a new bus station in Raven Meadows. *I Whitmarsh/ The Transport Museum, Wythall*

LEFT Veteran 4114, seen at Shrewsbury in 1971, entered service in January 1954 and would be the last D7 in passenger service when withdrawn in May 1973, although its last year or so was spent in the rather more strenuous environs of the Black Country. This particular D7 had a deeper windscreen. *Ken Jubb*

ABOVE RIGHT 1962 S15 5061 had been demoted from dual-purpose status by early 1968, and given traditional bus transfers. The wheels look suspiciously NBC grey but that horror is still a few years away; 5061 has encountered some country dirt – lighter than the city stuff! *Ken Jubb*

RIGHT The low bridge by the railway station was a major restriction on Midland Red activities, not least because double-deck buses were unable to take a direct route between the company's garage and the town centre. The introduction of 36 feet long single-deckers, initially in the form of LS18 Leyland Leopards and BMMO S17s, was particularly useful in Shrewsbury. Midland Red tested this manufacturer's demonstrator, SDU 930G seen by the offending bridge, a 36-feet long 1969 Daimler Fleetline SRG6-36 with Alexander two-door bodywork. When its demonstrating days around the UK had ended, this bus passed in 1973 to AA Motor Services (Dodds of Troon). *Ken Jubb*

RIGHT The T E Jones group went into liquidation and the services of its subsidiaries last operated on 2 September 1982, including Vagg of Knockin Heath, Oswestry, which ran into Shrewsbury. The Vagg stage services were replaced the next day by Crosville and Midland Red (North). The latter temporarily gave the ex-Vagg services a V prefix. Whereas Midland Red terminated its country services at Barker Street, Vagg had used Raven Meadows where Leyland National 537, new to Shrewsbury in August 1976, is seen on 2 August 1983.
Malcolm Keeley

BELOW Midland Red North set up a coach unit at Shrewsbury in 1983 and Leyland Leopard/Plaxton 681, new in January 1978 as a dual-purpose vehicle, was considered good enough to gain the Hotspur coach livery. It is seen at the garage on 2 August 1983.
Malcolm Keeley

STAFFORD

Opened: November 1921
To Midland Red North 6 September 1981
Closed: 2 February 1992

A small garage in Co-operative Street was owned by BMMO between July 1921 and July 1925 but it is not known if it was used before being let in 1922. A recently erected building on Pilgrim Place, just off Newport Road, was rented from November 1921 from Arthur Greatrex – a name that became very familiar in the town. Greatrex was already in the motor trade and his hire car business moved into coaches, expanding considerably after World War Two. BMMO purchased the Pilgrim Place premises in May 1925. The steel-framed, two-bay brick building could hold 16 vehicles, increased to 23 in March 1937 thanks to a slight extension.

Service expansion continued and the extra buses had to be open parked. Major reconstruction commenced in September 1960 following purchase of additional land and by 1962 the enlarged garage was capable of holding 57 buses. It now possessed the appearance of a post-war new build with a large new bay and office accommodation. In fact the original structural steelwork survived, the existing space having become the dock area.

The 1928 service renumbering allocated 821-878 to the Stafford, Cannock and Rugeley areas although 821-2 were poached for Lichfield. The S prefix for local services was introduced on 19 January 1946. While BMMO ran locals throughout the town itself, sister BET company Potteries Motor Traction (PMT) ran the routes to towns beyond the northern boundary. Stafford garage's longer services were therefore in the other directions such as Lichfield, Wolverhampton, Hednesford, Cannock, Bednall, Newport and Longridge.

For a time in Stafford, double-deck buses largely took over from saloons. BHA-registered FEDDs became numerous here while AD2 class AEC Regents were a notable non-BMMO type. The real celebrity vehicles, however, were the two D10s which worked out their remaining years here after their earlier trials around the system.

Stafford shared the 'Chaserider' brand, introduced here on 31 May 1980, with Cannock garage. Stafford's ex-Midland Red garage met a sudden end when fire engulfed the premises, destroying and damaging many vehicles so operations were moved to a new site.

ABOVE Buses unable to be housed inside the garage before its 1960s rebuilding were parked on rough ground later used for the extension. 1939 FEDD 2345 looks every day of its twenty years of age, despite the sunshine. Note the patching on the roof seams of the Brush body. *Ken Jubb*

ABOVE RIGHT This is the new exit to Pilgrim Place - vehicles now entering the garage through a new door via Espley's Yard. D5 3531 awaits a conductor and someone to attend to that open radiator cap. *Andrew Willis*

BELOW Interior of the extended garage in January 1962. Older buses and coaches are parked at the very rear – Midland Red kept its newer buses hard at work – while an Austin Cambridge staff car and a Land Rover are in the foreground. *BMMO*

RIGHT An unusual manoeuvre by Stafford garage was to use a coach on Monday to Friday peak bus journeys and here C1 3314 demonstrates its bus blinds. From 5 December 1964, Baswich services S81/2 were extended across town to Stone Road and Trinity Fields, absorbing PMT 215 and becoming a joint service with that operator. Midland Red took over the PMT workings from 11 March 1977 after the latter closed its small Stafford garage. *Ken Jubb*

BELOW RIGHT Stafford was home to 3241 for three years from the beginning of 1961. Seen loading in Newport Road, 3241 was one of the three 1948-9 S8s rebuilt with S15 fronts in 1957-8. *Andrew Willis*

ABOVE While many regarded Lichfield garage as the last resting place for Midland Red's buses, they actually moved on to breakers' yards particularly in Stafford. This sad scene in Snow's yard shows Leicester Southgate Street's tree cutter, DON prototype 1530, and ex-Oldbury D5 3478, immediately recognisable from the front with its opening vents in the front upper deck windows, the rear number box still displaying its last duty on Birmingham's Dudley Road services. *Andrew Willis*

BELOW After seeing rebuilt 3241 on the previous page, here's a genuine S15 - 4602 takes on board a formidable collection of lady shoppers in Rugeley, in the process blocking a Walsall Corporation Roe-bodied Leyland Titan PD2/12. *The Transport Museum, Wythall*

ABOVE 4 March 1965 was a freak weather day when Stafford was cut off from everywhere by snow for a few hours, even the West Coast main line was blocked for a time. Buses ran a much-truncated service and it was left to drivers to see how far out of town they could get. Photographed in Station Road around lunchtime is 1957 D7 4768 which spent its entire service career at Stafford until 1970 and then became a driver trainer. *Andrew Willis*

RIGHT The town became the home of the two underfloor-engine BMMO D10s after their trial period was over. 4943 has the style of fleetname and numbers adopted shortly before National Bus Company livery was imposed – the two D10s still carried the traditional colours when taken out of service in 1972-3. *Ken Jubb*

RIGHT Midland Red North was the last of the ex-Midland Red companies to remain in public ownership when Drawlane acquired it on 27 January 1988. A mainly white bus livery had been introduced in September 1987 which Drawlane instantly dispensed with after only 22 vehicles had been painted. Drawlane reintroduced Midland Red to the branding with this bright and practical livery. 1979 Leyland Leopard/ Plaxton 1427, with cherished registration 127 BPD in place of the original ELJ 211V, was acquired from fellow Drawlane subsidiary Shramrock & Rambler in August 1988 and was seen at Stafford on 12 May 1990. *Malcolm Keeley*

BELOW A low bridge under the West Coast Main Line at Little Haywood on the Stafford – Rugeley - Lichfield 825 service prevented the operation of Leyland Nationals with roof ventilation pods so Stafford received an allocation of National 2s which did not have them. Midland Red North lost its National 2s when Drawlane decided to concentrate the model with another subsidiary. Thus in 1988-9 a number of earlier Nationals had their pods removed and were renumbered into the 9xx series to highlight their availability for service 825. The former 701 is seen working another service in Stafford on 8 March 1994. MRN introduced new liveries in 1993, highly reminiscent of the old Midland Red, but unfortunately the shade was too dark and quickly looked drab when the sheen was lost. *Malcolm Keeley*

STOURBRIDGE

Opened: 22 July 1926

To West Midlands Passenger Transport Executive 3 December 1973

Closed: 26 January 1985

The new garage on the corner of St John's Road and Foster Street was not originally one of the company's most handsome structures, the steel frame being clad in metal sheeting instead of brick. It was, however, on an impressive site and its large forecourt became the town's bus station with a Booking and Enquiry Office. The garage could accommodate 47 vehicles after a small extension opened in July 1931.

The S prefix for local services was introduced here on 9 January 1936. Services further afield took Stourbridge buses to Birmingham, Kidderminster, Stourport, Bewdley, Cradley Heath, Dudley, Wednesbury, Kinver, Bridgnorth, Worcester, Bromsgrove and Wolverhampton. Increasing service requirements meant that a second bus station was opened across the road on the forecourt of Stourbridge Town railway station, catering for local and longer services to the south-west of the town. For many years a low railway bridge over Foster Street prevented double-deckers from these two bus stations working the busy 130 route through Halesowen, up Mucklow Hill to Birmingham. On 8 May 1948 a third bus station was opened in Vauxhall Road on the far side of the bridge, the 130 terminus being among those transferred there and thus permitting double-deckers, provided workings to and from the garage went a long way around. Accordingly the garage received a number of brand new AD2s, most remaining at the garage until withdrawal although more powerful buses later generally worked the 130. The road beneath the bridge was lowered in 1958.

The garage was reconstructed in 1958, being extended over the forecourt so that the buses terminating there now loaded under cover. Overnight, of course, the whole area was available for bus parking, increasing undercover capacity to 73. This was an improvement for passengers although the mixed-use problems of fumes and dirt, familiar at Birmingham's Digbeth coach station and Bull Ring bus station, would develop here on a smaller scale. Brick-built offices, workshops and an impressive Enquiry Office and Travel Bureau were built on the corner of the site.

Any journeys operated by the garage to destinations beyond the town boundary in the south-west direction were lost upon the PTE takeover (through journeys between Wolverhampton and Kidderminster were severed at Stourbridge) although, strangely, the service to Kinver in South Staffordshire remained at Stourbridge.

The railway line was eventually cut back to Stourbridge Town and the low bridge removed. Later still under the PTE, the line was slightly shortened further to allow the Town station and Vauxhall Road bus stations to be joined as one site, able to accommodate all bus services in Stourbridge, including those terminating in the garage. Work was spread widely within the PTE upon closure of the garage.

A mouth-watering view of Stourbridge garage and the 'Omnibus Station' on the forecourt in the 1930s. 1936 Metro-Cammell bodied FEDDs are present in quantity together with a couple of 1935 ONs and, to the right, a solitary 1931 IM4. *MRK collection*

ABOVE A pre-war view from the corner of the garage across the forecourt where FEDDs BHA 382 and HA 9448 of Dudley and Hartshill are loading. Over the road is the forecourt of Stourbridge Town station where an IM4 and a DON can be seen. *BMMO*

LEFT Stourbridge was home to most underfloor-engine single-deck types but a significant example was S4 prototype 1944 which spent most of its life working from this garage after wartime rebuilding from rear engine. However this is the S2 prototype 1942. *Gordon Davies*

ABOVE RIGHT The dock bay prior to the 1958 rebuild. The line-up includes two AD2s, 3110 and 3107, the former having had the top edge of its windscreen raised – a modification applied to all the early post-war double-deckers to improve visibility. Next to them, receiving fitters' attention, are FEDD 1854 with inspection light shining brightly and D5B 3822. *BMMO*

RIGHT D9 4922 tackles the short, sharp gradient to access the Kidderminster bus stands in the Town station forecourt. Across the road is the combined garage and bus station after the 1958 rebuild. The end of the office block, including the Enquiry Office and Travel Bureau, is on the left. No 4083, clearly identifiable as it was the only D7 to lose its front hopper ventilators, is leaving the garage on the 250 to Kinver, one of the traditional playgrounds for West Midlanders at holiday times. Stourbridge had a number of very early D7s from new – 4081-4/6. In the garage coaches can be seen parked by the side entrance from St John's Road. *The Transport Museum, Wythall*

The Friendly Midland Red

Alan Rowbotham was a driver at Stourbridge for many years but, in 1956, he was a 12-year old schoolboy with a camera interested in FEDD BHA 833. The foreman told him it was going for scrap that week. Also of interest was SON CHA 511 but it wouldn't start so Alan could not get a photo of that either. Alan thanked the foreman who suddenly invited him back with "Hang on a minute!"

The foreman returned with a cluster of drivers, conductors and mechanics. One driver clambered into the cab of CHA 511 while the rest pushed it out for Alan's schoolboy photo and then pushed it back. Reflect on Alan's treatment as a child when you regard the old slogan 'The Friendly Midland Red' with 21st century cynicism!

ABOVE One of the main beneficiaries of the loading stands covered over in the 1958 rebuild was the frequent service via Brierley Hill to Dudley of which around half the journeys were extended to Wednesbury. Journeys travelling the full distance were numbered 245 while the Dudley 'shorts' were 246. Hartshill garage provided most buses for the 245/6, although FEDD 2219 is associated with Stourbridge and behind is a GD6 Guy that must be on a working from Dudley garage. *MRK collection*

BELOW C1 3329 is parked near the St John's Road entrance on 25 May 1963. Black Country garages grievously felt the loss of the coaches which were all retained by Midland Red when the PTE took over. All Stourbridge had to offer enquirers was a BMMO S21. *Andrew Willis*

STRATFORD-UPON-AVON

Taken over from Stratford Blue 1 January 1971

To Midland Red South 6 September 1981

Closed: July 1990

Midland Red had many services into the internationally famous town so associated with William Shakespeare. However it did not have the Bard's home to itself. Stratford-upon-Avon Blue Motors was purchased from Midland General, part of the Balfour Beatty group, by Midland Red in 1935, just one of many smaller operators in its growth to become England's largest bus company. While a few were kept as subsidiaries for a short time, Stratford-upon-Avon Blue Motors remained a separate operating subsidiary for many years. Assisting continuity was Mr Walter Agg who had been in charge of Stratford Blue since 1931 and remained manager until passing away in 1958.

The British Electric Traction (BET) group was then owners of half the company buses in England and Wales, including Midland Red and thus Stratford Blue. It is true BET liked to keep a few small companies to give managers experience before moving them on to a larger operator but it is also pertinent that Stratford Blue staff, largely working through thin territory for passengers, had inferior pay rates and the little company could boast very low operating costs per mile. Midland Red finally

A good view of the signwriting over the door but the vehicle making its way out is a Northern General 1954 Guy Arab LUF touring coach with Gardner 6HLW engine and rare Picktree 35-seat coachwork. Many operators had arrangements with other companies to accommodate and provide cleaning facilities for tour coaches. *Ken Jubb*

absorbed Stratford Blue on 1 January 1971, not long after BET sold its bus interests to the state and, co-incidentally, the Stratford Blue pay rates had become those of Midland Red.

By this time, the Stratford Blue fleet of around 40 buses working from two garages (also see Kineton) ran not only Stratford's town services and country routes into the rural hinterland but also longer services as far as Birmingham, Cheltenham and Oxford. Its diverse territory through Warwickshire and Worcestershire, and into Gloucestershire and Oxfordshire, was one of the most beautiful in Britain.

If the retention of Stratford Blue was surprising enough, even more extraordinarily, Midland Red built buses were not normally supplied to the Stratford subsidiary which

LEFT The Stratford Blue subsidiary appeared completely independent of Midland Red. Although livery and lettering was simplified and modernised over the years, the Stratford Blue fleet always presented a traditional air. It was dependant in its earlier years on secondhand Tilling-Stevens buses; no 5 (WX 2120) dated from 1930 and was one of sixteen purchased from West Yorkshire Road Car in October 1938. It loads alongside the Red Lion and the garage is visible across the road. *R T Wilson/ The Transport Museum, Wythall*

BELOW LEFT Post-World War Two modernisation brought a fine fleet of Leylands, almost inevitably clad in Flowers brewery advertisements. The first Leyland double-deckers were Leyland-bodied PD2/1 models 32-39 (GUE 238-45), delivered in 1948 and the only ones for the company with half-drop ventilators. No 36 is seen in 1960, in the garage yard outside the offices. *Ken Jubb*

BELOW More PD2/1s followed in 1950, numbered 26-31 (JUE 354-9). This is no 26 passing through Stratford's market place in 1961. *Ken Jubb*

RIGHT An unusual activity for a BET subsidiary was Bridgetown Filling Station, owned by Stratford Blue since its earliest days as a private company. The service station was near the centre of Stratford, just across Clopton Bridge at the junction of the roads to Banbury and Oxford, and was sold in 1970. Stratford Blue also ran two chauffeur-driven Humber Pullman limousines from 1951 to 1962. Generally kept on the Bridgetown site was Stratford Blue's tree cutter, DHA 731, previously 1938 SON 2113 from the parent fleet and seen here in 1960. *Ken Jubb*

standardised initially on secondhand Tilling-Stevens vehicles. From 1948 new Leylands were almost exclusively bought instead, each painted in a smart blue and cream livery, with the double-deckers topped off by gleaming silver painted roofs until the mid-1960s.

The Stratford garage was prominently located in the town in Warwick Road, being completed for use in 1934. It was handily opposite the Red Lion whose yard was used for decades as Stratford's bus station, until 1986. The garage was considerably improved in the years immediately after World War Two with an extension allowing a total of around two dozen buses under cover. A new office block included an enquiry office overlooking a yard able to accommodate more buses.

Stratford had an allocation of 32 vehicles when Stratford Blue was absorbed into Midland Red on 1 January 1971. The NBC's Market Analysis Project, which endeavoured to ensure each garage could support itself financially by slimming the network until break-even was achieved, began with Midland Red. It eventually spread throughout NBC and to Scotland but the first MAP scheme (then known as the Viable Network Project) to reach fruition was at Stratford-upon-Avon, the revised network being branded 'Avonbus' from 28 May 1977.

Despite its 1971 disappearance in an era when company names are happily discarded in the waste bin by marketing experts, the name Stratford Blue has been revived several times by later organisations running the bus services of Shakespeare's world-famous town. Midland Red South itself revived it in May 1990, only two months before new premises on a trading estate just outside the town centre replaced the traditional garage which still exists.

RIGHT Most of Stratford Blue's 1950 Leyland Tiger PS2 chassis, previously carrying outdated half-cab single-deck bodies (see page 71), were rebodied as double-deckers. JUE 353 was the prototype, receiving in 1961 this graceless 63-seat body by Roe, incorporating Park Royal parts intended for AEC Bridgemasters. For a tiny operation, Stratford Blue's management seemed fleet and service number numskulls. In its rebodied form it was numbered 16, continuing the march backwards from no 39 begun in 1948 for double-deck buses. After the second generation 32-9 arrived in 1963, no 16 was renumbered 31 two years later. *Les Mason/ The Transport Museum, Wythall*

ABOVE Northern Counties supplied eight double-deck bodies in 1963, taking fleet numbers 32-39, previously carried by 1948 Titans. 36-9 were 73-seaters on new 30 feet long Leyland Titan PD3 chassis. 32-5 were shorter 63-seat bodies, mounted on 1950 Leyland Tiger PS2 chassis – this is no 33. *R Mallabon/ The Transport Museum, Wythall*

BELOW LEFT Willowbrook-bodied Leyland PD3s delivered at the very end of 1963 had fibreglass fronts and a new style of fleetname. Stratford Blue 3 (670 HNX) looks very new at Gloucester Green bus station, Oxford. Note that there was no longer a relief line between the off-white and the silver roof. Passengers on Stratford – Oxford service 44, jointly operated by Stratford Blue and City of Oxford, had to pay again as buses crossed the territorial boundary at Long Compton. This annoying practice finally ceased in 1964. It is notable that parent company Midland Red, having changed its mind after long experience of FEDD buses, continued to favour rear entrances on its front-engine double-deck buses. A number of operators adopted front entrances on thirty-footers so that the driver could take some responsibility for loading while the conductor handled the greater number of fares. Stratford Blue's services could not be described as crush-load urban so conductors were rarely under great pressure. Its territory, however, was very attractive so moving the entrances and staircases to the front was most unfortunate for lower deck riders whose forward vision was considerably hampered. *Ken Jubb*

ABOVE A further livery simplification was to delete the silver roofs altogether. Stratford Blue's three 1967 Leyland PDR1/1 Atlanteans with Northern Counties 75-seat bodies were not kept by Midland Red for long, being withdrawn in May 1971 and soon transferred to City of Oxford Motor Services. Here is no 10 during its brief period of Midland Red ownership. *Ken Jubb*

RIGHT At first glance looking like a D7 dressed for a Leicester service, 4725 is ready for a journey on ex-Stratford Blue local service L2. *Ken Jubb*

LEFT Stratford Blue's Leopards were repainted into Midland Red livery and most ran for several years while the Atlanteans, Titans and Tiger Cubs were soon sold – not to forget, although it is understandably hard to remember as they never turned a wheel in passenger service, the five new Leyland Panthers sold to Preston Corporation. 2057 was one of a 1964 pair of L2T Leopards with 41-seat Plaxton bodies and is seen at Coventry in 1972. It later spent some time at Evesham garage – its companion 2056 did some work at Worcester and Ludlow. They were retired at the end of the 1975 season. *Ken Jubb*

BELOW LEFT 2054 was a 1965 Leyland PSU3/3R with 53-seat body by Weymann and is seen working the ex-Stratford Blue Evesham-Cheltenham service, jointly operated with Bristol since 1931. 540 was a Midland Red service number associated with the Leamington area but it was Bristol who provided the identifications for this route which for many years was

numbered 64 or 64A depending on the villages served. It is newly repainted in this Spring 1971 view at Cheltenham; Midland Red at the time applied silver lettering to vehicles it considered were to dual-purpose or coach standard. *David Barber*

BELOW Among early repaints were two of the 1959 Leyland Tiger Cub/ Willowbrook buses, 2041 and 2043, but they did not last long as all the Tiger Cubs were withdrawn in April and May 1971. *Ken Jubb*

BOTTOM The entire ex-Stratford Blue Leyland Titan PD3 fleet was sold to Isle of Man Road Services in 1971-2 but not before most of them received Midland Red livery. This lucky shot shows 2024-2026 (536-8 EUE), three of the handsome 1963 Northern Counties-bodied PD3/4 models, together in the bus station. *Ken Jubb*

137

ABOVE 1977 Leyland National 625 at Shottery on 21 July 1984 passing Anne Hathaway's Cottage. *Yvonne Keeley*

RIGHT 12 July 1990 and the last days of this building as a bus garage. The Stratford Blue name had just undergone one of its periodic revivals, including the repainting of Leopard/ Plaxton no 4 (230 HUE). Now christened Rachel, no 4 had been new to Midland Red as 786 (BVP 786V) in July 1980 and MRS had upgraded it with a Leyland TL11 engine in 1985, later disguising its age with the cherished registration. Despite the tender loving care, Rachel looks unhappy with her front bumper. Alongside is 957 (YNA 329M), a 1974 Daimler Fleetline with Northern Counties body new to Greater Manchester, one of four purchased in 1988. *Malcolm Keeley*

SUTTON COLDFIELD

Opened: 27 August 1934

To West Midlands Passenger Transport Executive 3 December 1973

Closed: 8/9 January 1984

Although BMMO had services in the Royal Town of Sutton Coldfield from its earliest days, a garage in the town was not provided until 1934. The four-bay steel frame red brick structure on Upper Holland Road was classic Midland Red in style but its original capacity of 60 vehicles was soon inadequate. With many shortages making life difficult, an extension to the rear of this garage opened on 31 January 1950, increasing the capacity to 100, was the first to be achieved by the company after World War Two.

Very important were the services from Birmingham through Sutton or New Oscott to places like Streetly, Mere Green and beyond. Some continued through Tamworth, Lichfield and Burton to Nottingham and Derby although other garages contributed to these longer routes. The town enjoyed a considerable network of local routes - the S prefix being introduced on 27 September 1937. Some of these reached across the border into Erdington, Birmingham.

Sutton Coldfield Town Council for many years insisted on single-deck buses only and Tilling-Stevens TTA2 buses, O 9937-42, delivered in May-June 1913, were the first single-deckers in the BMMO fleet. They would prove unusual for Midland Red in having rear entrance bodies - 27-seaters bodied by Birch. The garage was built to double-deck height and FEDDs from the original HA 94xx series were used on service 107 to Birmingham via New Oscott but it would be 1938, after several traffic court hearings, before double-deckers entered general use in Sutton Coldfield. Perhaps it was revenge that caused BMMO to divert the FEDDs during World War Two and replace them with the rough-and-ready wartime austerity Guys plus elderly AEC Regents hired from London Transport! Perhaps it was simply a recognition that rear-entrance buses handled busy services better. Standard BMMO types formed the post-war fleet until the Fleetline era – there were a lot of D5s here, including 3523-9.

The proudly independent borough was forced into Birmingham on 1 April 1974. In PTE days, Sutton received many Volvo Ailsas. Upon closure a few of these joined the Ailsas at Oldbury but most went with work to the ex-Birmingham City Transport garage at Perry Barr. The rest of the work passed to other ex-BCT garages and the ex-municipal bus garage at Walsall.

The garage in 1973. *Ken Jubb*

LEFT 1950 Brush-bodied S12 3745 is seen in the centre of Sutton while working a local. A cut and shut repair has been carried out on the grille, judging by the abbreviated number of slots *Ken Jubb*

BELOW LEFT The yard of Sutton garage in 1952 is host to 1618 (AHA 513), new in 1935 as diesel engines were becoming popular. It belonged to the last batch of petrol-engine single-deckers, the ON class, although petrols were fitted to coaches and double-deckers for a while longer. Some of these ONs were converted to compression ignition engines (as diesels were then referred to) in 1938 as the CON class, including 1618. Nudd reconditioned its Short Bros 38-seat body in 1949, allowing it to run until 1956. *Gordon Davies*

BELOW The fifty 1937 SOS SLRs had 30-seat coachwork by English Electric. Contemporary new buses by this time were diesel powered but, like many operators, petrol engines continued to be specified in coaches because of their smoother running. These were the last petrol coaches for BMMO, however, and were converted to Leyland E181 7.4 litre diesels in 1947-8. They were being refurbished at this time after World War Two, receiving fresh upholstery and externally facelifted with new grilles and styling mouldings, no 1980 (CHA 962) on page 19 being typical. No 2001 (CHA 983) was one of a few, however, rebuilt more extensively, losing the tapered window pillars, and gaining plain wheelarches and bumpers front and rear. The SLRs were all sold in 1955 apart from the pair converted to trainee vehicles. *Gordon Davies*

RIGHT 1938 FEDD 2120, with Brush body renovated at Hooton during 1951, stands in the garage in 1960. *Ken Jubb*

BELOW RIGHT One of the many wartime Guys allocated to Sutton, in this case 2560 (HHA 12) dating from 1944. Its body is by Weymann prior to the major rebuilding applied to these vehicles in 1950-1. *The Transport Museum, Wythall collection*

SWADLINCOTE

Opened: 19 September 1931

To Midland Red East 6 September 1981; relaunched as Midland Fox January 1984. To Stevensons August 1987, relaunched as Arriva 1997

Closed: 24 December 2007

The Burton & Ashby Light Railway was actually a tramway but was railway owned. Railway practices prevailed, the tramway enjoying its own right of way across the fields. This missed a lot of intermediate housing, providing bus operators with an opportunity to compete. BMMO joined in via Swadlincote and contributed the final knock-out blow to the tramway which closed on 19 February 1926.

Land was purchased from the London Midland & Scottish Railway Co in 1931 on which BMMO built its garage in Midland Road, Swadlincote. The steel-framed building was clad in sheeting, with offices and workshops in brick. There was a small amount of space for open parking, enlarged after further land was purchased from the British Transport Commission in 1951. The garage had accommodation for 39 vehicles, and workaday services around Burton, "Swad", Ashby-de-la-Zouch and Measham was its bread and butter. There were longer services, however, taking Swadlincote vehicles to Birmingham and Nuneaton for example.

The arrival of FEDDs in 1945 were the first permanent allocation of double-deck buses at Swadlincote and soon numerous AD2s were there too. Swadlincote was an early recipient of Leyland Leopards, beginning with new LS18s allocated from 1962-3.

Swadlincote became part of the 'Lancer' network with Coalville, introduced on 17 February 1979, the branding being dropped at the first opportunity after the split when Swadlincote services were revised and renumbered 191-9 from 27 February 1982. Double-deck buses returned to the garage at this time but, in complete contrast, 'Fox Cub' minibuses were introduced to Ashby in March 1986 and Burton in April. Midland Red North's unsuccessful attempt at minibus operation in Lichfield was taken over on 13 April 1987.

Midland Fox was privatized on 19 August 1987 with a management buyout obtaining the majority and Stevensons a 40% shareholding. As part of the deal, Stevensons acquired Swadlincote garage with the Swadlincote and Lichfield operations. This included 32 almost new 'Fox Cub' Ford Transits along with a dozen large buses.

S17 5770 in one of the garage entrances with a glimpse of the side yard.
E C Tuff/ BMMO, courtesy Kithead Trust

ABOVE Swadlincote received its first double-deckers in 1945. The early arrivals were FEDDs from the FHA 2xx series, new in 1938-9 and including 2242, although later FEDD stock included some BHAs and EHAs. 2242 is seen shortly after rebuilding of its Brush body at Hooton in 1951. *Roy Marshall*

LEFT 1966 Fleetline 6028 had a second career as a driver training bus with Midland Fox until sale in February 1990. Visible in the background is HWY 722N, one of several Alexander-bodied Leyland Leopards purchased by Fox from West Riding. *Malcolm Keeley*

BELOW Swadlincote's yard on 17 August 1985 contains 2641 (MLK 641L), one of Midland Fox's massive fleet of ex-London Daimler Fleetlines. *Malcolm Keeley*

TAMWORTH TWOGATES

Opened: 1 February 1918
Closed: 2 August 1928

The town of Tamworth has a long history with its castle but more recently its residents have been involved in coalmining, textiles, paper, brick and terra cotta production, market gardening and not forgetting Reliant cars. The North Warwickshire Motor Omnibus & Traction Company, Ltd, one of BMMO's sister companies within the BET, got into difficulties during World War One and, from 1 February 1918, Midland Red buses started to work what remained of its network of services out of Nuneaton and Twogates, near Tamworth. This included the garage in Watling Street, Twogates, where the acquired vehicles were gradually

Staff and part of Twogate's vehicle allocation in 1922. HA 2326 is exceptionally interesting, being a Garford 15-seater. O 9937 was one of the ex-War Department Tilling-Stevens TS3 lorry chassis, lengthened to 15-feet wheelbase, given a recycled registration from a Tilling TTA2 and entering service with a new bus body in 1921. OH 1204 and OE 6170 are more TS3 Tillings, new to BMMO in 1920.
The Transport Museum, Wythall, collection

replaced by Midland Red stock, including a Garford. Twogates was replaced by the garage in Aldergate but not disposed of until 1947 when the North Warwickshire company was wound up.

TAMWORTH ALDERGATE

Opened: 3 August 1928
To Midland Red North 6 September 1981, relaunched as Arriva 1997
Still in use

This was another classic inter-war steel-frame red brick garage, this time holding around forty buses, and including an Enquiry Office. Its central location in Aldergate has been ideal for the terminating services around the corner. An extension was opened in February 1957. Double-deck buses were introduced after World War Two but non-BMMO types did not feature until the arrival of the LS18 single-deckers. The latter included some dual-purpose versions as the garage contributed to the X99 Birmingham - Nottingham service.

Most of the garage's activities, however, were various routes to Birmingham, the 765 Lichfield – Coventry service, and local services in Tamworth and Atherstone. The 1928 service renumbering allocated 776-820 to Tamworth and Atherstone although 810-22 were actually used in the Burton and Lichfield areas. There were, however, also some colliery services for which the C prefix was used from 17 May 1958. The town considerably expanded in the latter part of 20th century, strengthening its links with the West Midlands conurbation but remaining outside the PTE area.

Midland Red used few of the buses taken over with Whieldon's Green Bus of Rugeley on 5 November 1973 but several relatively modern Seddon Pennines were placed in service at Tamworth.

'Mercian' local branding was introduced on 1 September 1979. Minibuses, initially Freight Rovers, took over certain services from 11 August 1986. Tamworth opened the 1990s in the precarious position of being at the centre of a retaliatory bus war with Derby City Transport. This ended on 18 February 1990 when MRN sold its entire Derby allocation of minibuses, all Freight Rovers, to the City Transport.

ABOVE Four modern Leyland Leopard coaches obtained in 1983 by Midland Red North were later repainted and fitted out for Midland Express bus services. Two were 1982 Leopards with ECW coachwork and were seen at Tamworth garage on 17 May 1987. They were ex-Southern Vectis 1501 (RDL 308X) and ex-National Travel (West) 1502 (ANA 91Y). *Malcolm Keeley*

BELOW 1976 Leyland Leopard no 450, with Plaxton Supreme body to bus grant specification, passes the garage on 1 March 1979. On the end of the building is the Enquiry Office, at this time carrying NBC branding and describing itself as a Travel Centre. *E V Trigg*

LEFT A look inside the garage in June 1959 reveals 1947 S6 3057.
F W York/ The Transport Museum, Wythall

BELOW LEFT The old wheel and tyre motif remains above the Enquiry Office in 1968 but all the printed material has the new underlined fleetname and the stuffy formality of earlier advertising has gone.
BMMO

BELOW No 2372, loading at Tamworth bus station, was one of the last six pre-war buses in service, all FEDD types being withdrawn on the last day of 1960; the others were 2219/28/54, 2358/81.
Ken Jubb

RIGHT 5193 spent its entire life working from Tamworth. It was new in August 1963 as one of the twenty Willowbrook-bodied Leyland Leopards finished to dual-purpose standard with 48 seats for prestige duties and classified LS18A. Tamworth primarily used it on the X99 Birmingham – Nottingham service. 5193 was later reseated to 53 bus seats as an ordinary LS18 and is seen here on a local service. It ran until March 1978. *Ken Jubb*

BELOW RIGHT The 806/7 to Leyfields estate were introduced on 25 July 1964 and later extended to Coton Green. D7 4539 is seen in Tamworth Bus Station in 1969. *Ken Jubb*

LEFT One of the Seddons taken over from Green Bus was no 2150, a 1972 Pennine VI with Plaxton 53-seat coachwork, here parked in the approach road that leads to the side entrance of the garage on 24 July 1977. It was sold in 1978. *Garry Yates*

BELOW National Bus Company's poppy red was frequently teased as uninteresting while Midland Red North's idea of extending the local identity colours from paper publicity to branding stripes on the poppy vehicles themselves would seem to have been asking for trouble. In reality the combinations looked stunning, arguably working in every branding shade. A colourful collection on 21 March 1987 is led by 1973 Leopard/ Marshall 244 in poppy red with Mercian green branding stripe. Behind is one of Midland Red North's twenty ex-London DMS class Leyland-engined Fleetlines, all acquired from Western National. No 1927 with Park Royal 73-seat body dated from 1974 and was one of the final ten acquired in October 1986 that were placed on the road in green livery. Tamworth garage was perhaps chosen because the colour matched the branding of the town's buses. The huge cuts of April 1987 saw off all the DMSs meaning few of the later acquisitions made it into red livery. At the rear is a Freight Rover minibus in the yellow and green livery applied to those allocated to Tamworth. *Malcolm Keeley*

WELLINGTON

Opened: 21 July 1932

To Midland Red North 6 September 1981, relaunched as Arriva 1997

Closed: 15 April 2012

The first Midland Red buses in the town, from 1922, were worked from Shrewsbury garage. The company's first garage here was in Mansell Road and was rented from the Wellington Transport Co from 9 July 1926. The original fleet of three buses grew rapidly, their maintenance being the responsibility of Shrewsbury until the new garage on Charlton Street was opened. BMMO had a large underground petrol storage tank installed at Mansell Road as late as 1931, perhaps at the insistence of the local authority. The plans show the supporting construction included chassis sides supplied by BMMO to the builder, presumably from withdrawn Tillings.

The 1932 replacement steel-framed and sheeted structure on Charlton Street could hold fifteen buses. The allocation began to expand rapidly in the early post-war years and the extra vehicles were parked on adjoining land.

A basically new garage replaced the original on the same site, opening in September 1953 and capable of holding 50 vehicles although the allocation at the time was 39. The new garage now occupied Charlton Street almost to Vineyard Road, the original

garage having been located in what was now the right-hand side. While the sides were mostly sheeted, the brick frontage of the steel-framed garage was very modern looking for its time, introducing some of the styling features that would become familiar on the company's many new building projects over the next decade. A former orchard along the stretch of Charlton Street leading to Queen Street later provided space for parking five buses plus cars belonging to staff.

Midland Red did not operate double-deck buses from Charlton Street, being very much a home for BMMO single-deckers during the period they were built. On the Wellington allocation for much of their lives were the experimental LA 3977 and prototype S14 4178.

The 1928 service renumbering reserved 898-925 for the Wellington and Oakengates areas although the numbers eventually crept back to 894. The garage worked services from the town to Shrewsbury, Wolverhampton, Bridgnorth and Kidderminster,

Staff at Wellington in 1934. *The Transport Museum, Wythall/ courtesy D E Evans*

Madeley, Ironbridge, Much Wenlock, Oakengates, Market Drayton, and numerous smaller places. 'All around the Wrekin', referring to the well-known hill, is an expression commonly used by Midlanders to describe any sort of circuitous route but is a fair assessment of Wellington garage's operating territory. The W prefix was introduced for local services from 30 June 1947.

The development of Telford new town drastically changed the area. The 'Tellus' branding was introduced on 1 April 1978 following the takeover of the bus operations of seven independents in the Shropshire Omnibus Association and a fleet of new Leyland Nationals, 683-702, was allocated to Wellington for these services. The rural services worked from Wellington, however, were soon rebranded as part of the Shropshire 'Hotspur' network introduced on 24 November 1979. The 'Tellus' services were recast and renumbered in September 1981. They received minibuses from 19 April 1986. The garage was replaced by new premises in Telford.

ABOVE Wellington's Booking and Enquiry Office was in Queen Street, just around the corner from the garage. Seen outside is 1938 English Electric-bodied SON 2182 about to work the 941 service to Little Wenlock via Horsehay. *Michael Rooum*

BELOW The 1953 rebuilding included a bus loading bay on the corner of Vineyard Road at the request of the council, intended to reduce the instances of Charlton Street being impeded by buses loading with passengers. *BMMO*

ABOVE RIGHT Wellington gets a visit from Digbeth's CL3 class 4233 in 1966. This was one of seventeen 1954 C3 coaches fitted with new Plaxton Panorama 36-seat touring coach bodies, mostly in 1962. *Ken Jubb*

RIGHT The garage and its side yard are visible behind S16 5107 in late 1973. Traditional livery and fleetnames are still carried by 5107, albeit somewhat faded, but NBC grey wheel policy has already been imposed. *David Barber*

RIGHT The development of Telford brought additional variants to the X96 route, including the X94 between Coventry and Wellington. The BMMO S22s may have boasted 45 dual-purpose seats but lacked the imagination of the Sinclair years as nothing about the styling or bland livery indicated anything special. Wellington's 5882, new at the beginning of 1968, passes through Dudley in 1970.
Ken Jubb

BELOW Wellington garage provided Bridgnorth's town services, originally introduced on 18 April 1953. A new Midland Red North Leyland Tiger, no 1707, was at work in High Town on 1 June 1984, the Duple 51-seat bodies on these had to have the coloured band below the windows because of the shallow roof contour.
Malcolm Keeley

WOLVERHAMPTON BILSTON STREET

Opened: 14 May 1920
Closed: 1 March 1964

The BET-owned Wolverhampton District Electric Tramways depot at Sedgley was briefly used from 13 December 1919 as a base for new operations in the Black Country until they were transferred to these leased former livery stables. The freehold was purchased in June 1920 when its official capacity was 24 vehicles, later reduced to 21 due to its awkward interior as vehicles got bigger. This was a small garage bearing in mind Wolverhampton was a large industrial town, later given city status, but was not as tiny as it looked because the bulk of the steel-framed brick structure spread behind gabled brick buildings used as offices by the company, including an Enquiry Office. There were two entrance/ exits of which only one was raised to allow double-deck buses.

It is the latter that has provided the rolling stock interest. The wartime AEC Regents ran here until 1949 when the Leyland TD7s of similar vintage displaced them. When

Bilston Street garage with 1936 SON 1926 (CHA 550) parked outside. The entrance increased in height to permit double-deck buses is clearly visible. Next along the street is the Enquiry Office then, above the SON's emergency door, is the large sign NO ENTRANCE DOUBLE-DECK advertising the location of the other vehicle entrance. Finally there are more company offices. *Michael Rooum*

the LD8s arrived in 1953, the double-deck fleet was briefly entirely Leyland until the TD7s began to be withdrawn.

The garage provided buses for services to Stourbridge and contributed to the Birmingham – Wolverhampton – Stafford group. More locally it served areas such as Bilston, Wednesbury, Darlaston, Willenhall, Sedgley, Tipton, Great Bridge, Hurst Hill and Oldbury.

These were veteran premises on the BMMO system that never quite shook off their equine origins and the replacing Dudley Road garage was quite a contrast.

WOLVERHAMPTON DUDLEY ROAD

Opened: 1 March 1964

Closed: 1 October 1971

Nothing demonstrates the rapid decline of the company's fortunes better than the short life of this excellent garage, constructed in reinforced concrete with steel framing and brickwork walling. It was sited on the junction of Dudley Road and Grove Street, with its entrance on Birmingham Road and exit on Dudley Road. The garage included a Booking and Enquiry Office and a unique feature for Midland Red was an employees' underground car park. Five inspection pits with underfloor heating were provided. The official capacity was 60 vehicles but the maximum allocated was 32. The era of severe service economies was soon here and the garage closed - work passing to Dudley, Oldbury, Stourbridge, Stafford and Wellington.

ABOVE The last days at Wolverhampton in 1971. *Ken Jubb*

BELOW A revised network in the Bilston and Darlaston area, effective from 3 December 1966, saw services 273-80/5/7 in the Black Country series of numbers replaced by the 861-4/7. S17 5566 is seen on one of the later routes early in 1971. *Ken Jubb*

WORCESTER EAST STREET

Opened: 7 September 1914
Closed: 28 May 1971

Worcester's buses were originally worked from the tramcar depot. The motorbus assets of the Worcester and Kidderminster tramway companies were passed to the Worcestershire Motor Transport Company, Ltd., on 14 August 1914. The intention was to combine and develop these bus interests and, with expansion, WMT began leasing East Street. WMT, however, suffered the majority of its vehicles being requisitioned by the War Office and BMMO took over in November 1914. It is recorded that BMMO initially housed buses in the St John's tramway depot, despite the availability of East Street. One can only speculate that much of East Street was taken up with bodies removed from the requisitioned chassis. BMMO mounted these bodies on new Tilling-Stevens chassis and ran some from East Street, alongside others with double-deck bodies. Affairs were tidied up with the transfer of East Street garage from WMT to Midland Red in April 1921.

East Street garage was an extraordinary place, made of corrugated iron and originally a roller skating rink, described in Midland Red's own staff magazine as a 'queer old building'. While staff could enter the garage at the front, vehicle access was at the rear via a yard to the side. The company in 1923 erected a foreman's house in Washington Street, abutting East Street garage. Chief Engineer Shire justified the expenditure with the remark 'It will be very advantageous for us to have our Foreman on the spot at our beck and call, any time, day or night'.

The garage was extended in 1924 but was totally inadequate to accommodate the tramway replacement buses introduced in 1928

and became a dormitory shed of the large additional premises in Padmore Street. East Street was used regularly until March 1930 and then used for storage etc before being let to Worcester Corporation from 1936 for use as a fruit and vegetable market, partly reverting to Midland Red in 1946 and the remainder in 1949. Around thirty buses were accommodated there overnight until 1962, the premises again being reduced to non-operational status but retained with platform staff tuition roles and as the South Division Body Shop, capable of dealing with three vehicles at a time. It was finally vacated on 28 May 1971 and sold later that year.

ABOVE The 'queer old building' on East Street in 1971. *Ken Jubb*

BELOW The rear of East Street garage in June 1927. *BMMO*

WORCESTER PADMORE STREET

Opened: 31 May 1928

To Midland Red West 6 September 1981, relaunched as First in November 2001

Still in use

An enormous influx of new buses into the Midland Red fleet in 1928 was both a reflection of ongoing replacement of Tilling-Stevens TS3 buses and important service developments, most particularly in Worcester. The Corporation had the right to purchase the city's tramways, operated by the BET-owned Worcester Electric Traction Co Ltd, 28 years after 1 May 1901. The Corporation obtained powers in 1926 to acquire the tramways, convert them to trolleybus or motorbus operation, and run buses on many roads outside the city. The Corporation accordingly acquired the tramways company and the General Manager of Birmingham Corporation Tramways, acting as consultant, recommended conversion to trolleybuses with supplementary motorbus services. Ignoring consultants' advice was evidently just as popular then as, instead of operating its own buses, an agreement was entered into whereby BMMO would operate all the city services on behalf of the Corporation for 21 years, with an option for renewal. BMMO would pay to the Corporation the net profits on all routes passing through the city on a proportionate route mileage basis for the portion of the route within the city. The last trams ran on 31 May 1928 with Midland Red buses taking over the next day. The successful agreement formed the basis of most other subsequent agreements between the company and local authorities and was widely adopted by other operators. The replacing buses included new QL models HA 3725-55 and the bus routes saw the first use of the prefixed local service numbers, in this case W, of course.

Two land purchases alongside each other on Padmore Street were made in 1927 in readiness for the enlarged fleet. BMMO purchased land and an engineering factory previously known as Vulcan Works from the Westinghouse Brake and Saxby Signal Co, London. The secondhand premises lacked the flair of the company's own designs and comprised several short bays in steel-framed corrugated iron with many roof stanchions to hamper flow. Offices and workshops were included within the main structure.

Accommodation for at least twelve more buses was immediately required but the second of the 1927 land purchases was available, being former railway sidings at the Cromwell Street end of Padmore Street, previously owned by the Vinegar Works, Lowesmoor. An extension opened in 1930 was built on this land and was suitable for fully enclosed double-deckers although, interestingly, such buses were not favoured by BMMO at the time, increasing total capacity to around seventy vehicles. A mess room added in 1938 was

ABOVE The LRR service coaches and OLR touring vehicles were relegated to bus services during World War Two. The OLRs were extensively rebuilt from normal to forward control to permit 34 seats, a useful increase of five, but retained the petrol engines specified when new in 1935. No 1690 has terminated at Hereford's Bus Station while working the 417 via Ledbury. *MRK collection*

LEFT A superb view of Padmore Street around 1953 showing a D5B taking advantage of one of the two bays constructed later and capable of accommodating double-deck buses. The 1938 mess room can be seen nearest the camera with the railway line to a former siding disappearing beneath it. *BMMO*

built over the disused railway line. Like elsewhere on the system, Worcester's allocation grew, reaching nearly 100 in the post-war peak including vehicles kept at the East Street and Malvern dormitory sheds. Opening of the new Malvern garage in 1954 eased pressure on Padmore Street. The company began purchasing land adjacent to Padmore Street with an intention of replacing it and East Street with a new garage but this plan was stalled by the City Council's thoughts for a relief road over the site. The large area of land thus became available for open parking so East Street was closed but Padmore Street has not been replaced to date.

The cathedral city of Worcester was an important area for the company and the 1928 renumbering reserved 352-421 for non-local services around Worcester, Malvern and Evesham. A large proportion of the allocation was single-deckers for both rural and city services. Services ran through Worcester from Birmingham in one direction to Gloucester and Cheltenham in the other. Rural services took Worcester's buses to Hereford, Kidderminster, Stourbridge, Pershore, Evesham and countless villages.

The introduction of driver only operation at Worcester was achieved on 23 March 1963 but had been a painful experience for management and platform staff. Several years of negotiations had included strikes on several Saturdays in early 1962 when free replacement bus services were organised by a frustrated Worcester Chamber of Commerce and the People's League for the Defence of Freedom. Non-BMMO types did not make an impact here until the mid-1960s.

Some pillars and support beams were modified in the 1960s to make more of the garage suitable for double-deck buses, including access to more maintenance pits. The city services were considerably revised on 1 July 1967 including the introduction of double-deck buses on certain routes using new Daimler Fleetlines 6046-55. 'Severnlink' branding was introduced on 13 January 1979 but ceased from July 1984.

Large scale operation of minibuses by Midland Red West began on 23 November 1985 when sixty Mercedes-Benz L608D minibuses were introduced to Worcester in a special livery, carrying the fleetname 'Citibus' and the city's coat-of-arms on the sides. Most services in the Malvern area were converted to minibuses from 1 April 1989; Worcester garage receiving some ex-Southdown Mercs to increase its stock. A second generation of Mercs in the form of Varios arrived in 1998 but a new manager concluded that minibuses were too small ever to make a satisfactory profit.

ABOVE Until 1946, Angel Place was the main terminal for Midland Red country services. Congestion became critical and, in December 1945, Midland Red and Worcester Corporation met to see what could be done. It is to the credit of everybody involved at that most difficult time just after World War Two that a properly designed and equipped bus and coach station was provided in six months in Newport Street and officially opened on 15 July 1946. The bus station and its shelters were owned by Worcester Corporation. S9 3419 in 1964 is about to work the 372 which was a collector's item for route enthusiasts as it did something different every day! It ran as far as Bishops Frome, Bromyard or Herefordshire House on certain days, with short workings to Acton Green, Suckley or Alfrick. *Ken Jubb*

LEFT Midland Red buses served all but the smallest villages in Middle England, many with romantic names that sing out across the centuries. Worcester's blinds, of which the top version is seen here, includes some of the most delightful, including White Ladies Aston that probably gets today's politically correct lobby foaming at the mouths in almost every respect. The blinds of Black Country garages included many of the most attractive destinations on the company's network, these summer extras providing a welcome change for their crews. *Destination blind copyright R J Williamson*

ABOVE RIGHT The M5 opened on 20 July 1962 and Midland Red began its Birmingham-Worcester express service X44 the same day, reducing the time between the two cities from 93 to 50 minutes, faster than the rail service. CM5s 4833-5 from Worcester and 4836-7 from Digbeth were used but, unlike the London CM5T vehicles, these did not have toilets and could seat 37. Later a service variant routed via Bearwood was introduced as the X43. The original coaches were replaced by CM6 vehicles in 1966, seating 46 compared to the 44 of the more usual CM6T. One of these, 5669, loads at Newport Street. *Ken Jubb*

RIGHT The X72/3/4 between Birmingham and Gloucester/ Cheltenham last ran on 31 December 1971, being replaced south of Worcester by new services. Leopard/ Marshall 319 is seen at Tewkesbury on 10 June 1978 in the company of Bristol's LH 370. *Malcolm Keeley*

The November 1985 introduction of minibuses did not help the city's traffic congestion but brought increased frequencies, reduced waiting times and thus a perception of greater reliability. This was the first major use of Mercedes-Benz by a National Bus Company operator, previously Ford Transits had been the favourite manufacturer elsewhere. Midland Red West's Mercs were converted to bus use by several bodybuilders, Worcester's 1329 was by Robin Hood and seated 20. This view dates from 31 March 1988. *Malcolm Keeley*